Hermine Kiehnle · Monika Graff
Original Schwäbisch
The Best of Swabian Food

HÄDECKE

Hermine Kiehnle · Monika Graff

Original Schwäbisch
The Best of
Swabian Food

Kulinarische Texte
von
Josef Thaller

ISBN 978-3-7750-0622-4
aktualisierte Neuausgabe
4 | 2015
Printed in Germany 2015
© 1996, 2002, 2012 Hädecke Verlag GmbH & Co. KG
71256 Weil der Stadt
www.haedecke-verlag.de

Abbildung Vor- und Nachsatz aus
EMAIL von Brigitte ten Kate von Eicken

Picture endpapers from
EMAIL von Brigitte ten Kate von Eicken

Übersetzung ins Englische: Lyra Turnbull
Fotos: Chris Meier, Stuttgart
Umschlaggestaltung: Julia Graff
Typografie und Satz: ES Typo-Graphic,
Ellen Steglich, Stuttgart

English translation: Lyra Turnbull
Photographs: Chris Meier, Stuttgart
Cover design: Julia Graff
Typography and typesetting:
ES Typo-Graphic, Ellen Steglich, Stuttgart

In derselben Reihe erschienen/published in the same series:
Original Badisch – The Best of Baden Food, ISBN 978-3-7750-0416-9
Original Bayrisch – The Best of Bavarian Food, ISBN 978-3-7750-0478-7
Original Fränkisch – The Best of Franconian Food, ISBN 978-3-7750-0662-0
Original Hessisch – The Best of Hessian Food, ISBN 978-3-7750-0583-8
Original Pfälzisch – The Best of Palatine Food, ISBN 978-3-7750-0471-8
Original Sächsisch – The Best of Saxon Food, ISBN 978-3-7750-0494-7

Abkürzungen	Abbreviations
kg – Kilogramm	lb – pound(s)
g – Gramm	oz – ounce(s)
l – Liter	pt – pint(s)
ml – Milliliter	tbsp – tablespoon(s)
EL – Esslöffel	tsp – teaspoon(s)
TL – Teelöffel	cm – centimetre(s)
cm – Zentimeter	mm – millimetres(s)
mm – Millimeter	

Die Rezepte sind – soweit nicht anders angegeben – für 4 Portionen.

If not otherwise indicated, the recipes yield 4 servings.

Rezepte

Recipes

Das Originale wird immer seltener. Es ist, wie alle Merkmale regionaler Identität am Entschwinden. Verdrängt von einer immer mehr um sich greifenden Globalisierung, die mit ihren Gleichschaltungsmechanismen auch die letzten Winkel der Erde erreicht hat. Es gibt ein paar Ecken die bisher noch ausgespart blieben, aber dies ist wohl eher zufällig und irgendwann werden auch die letzten Refugien von McDonald & Co. eingenommen werden.

Dabei übt gerade heute das Originale eine nie zuvor gekannte Anziehungskraft aus. Nostalgiekranke und kindheitssehnsüchtige Esser machen kilometerlange Umwege um noch in den Genuss handgeschabter Spätzle zu kommen. Was vor einem halben Jahrhundert noch undenkbar gewesen wäre, denn es gab keine anderen als handgeschabte Spätzle.

Es sind wohl allein die schwäbischen Spätzle und der bayerische Kartoffelknödel, die bisher noch einer Verfremdung trotzten. Zwei letzte Bastionen gegen die Veränderungswut unserer Zeit. Am meisten müssen unter diesem Wahn die schwäbischen Maultaschen leiden. Selbst in Dorfgaststätten gibt es mittlerweile Maultaschen die mit Lachs statt wie es sich gehört mit Kalbsbrät und Spinat gefüllt werden. Andere Originale der schwäbischen Küche, wie das „Beugel" entschwanden schon Anfang des letzten Jahrhunderts auf Nimmerwiedersehen und es tauchte unvermutet als „Bagel" in der neuen Welt, zuerst in Toronto, später in New York wieder auf und feiert seither in den dortigen Metropolen Triumphe. Das „Beugel" war neben der Fastenbrezel eines der beliebtesten Fastengebäcke und wurde von den zur „Purifizierung" vor Ostern eine Beichte ablegenden „Beichtgehern" den Daheimgebliebenen vom Bäcker mitgebracht. Besonders beliebt hierbei war das „Brezel- und Beugel-

reißen", wenn die Brezel oder Beugel nicht für alle reichten.

Das Beugel war ein originales Brauchtumsgebäck und dies ist wohl auch die Erklärung für sein Entschwinden. Mit dem Entschwinden des Brauchtums ist auch das Gebäck entschwunden.

Bei manchen Originalen kann auch nicht so ohne weiteres die „Ausschließlichkeit", die ja das Merkmal jeden Originals ist, beansprucht werden. Sie haben ein Pendant auf der anderen Seite des Zauns. So die „Bubaspitzle" in den fränkischen „Wargele" oder „Bauchstecherle" oder die „sauren Rädle" im bayerischen „sauren Kartoffelgemüas". Selbst etwas so urschwäbisches wie der „Gaisburger Marsch", dessen Entstehung bei Thaddäus Troll belegt ist, hat ein österreichisches Militärgegenstück, den „Grenadiermarsch". Ein von den Zutaten, wie auch der Zubereitung her identisches Gericht. Bis auf die Spätzle. Die österreichischen Militärköche haben bei diesem traditionellen Samstagsgericht, das nichts anderes als ein „Marsch durch die Wochenreste" war und vor allem der Verwendung übriggebliebenen Rindfleischs diente, statt der Spätzle Nudeln genommen.

Die Spätzle jedenfalls, diese seltsamen und eigenwilligen Teiggebilde werden sich weiter behaupten. Sie werden, wie schon im Vorwort zum Vorgängerband dieses Buches angemerkt: „das einzige Produkt sein, das die Schwaben im 21. Jahrhundert noch genau so machen wie vor 700 Jahren".

Authentizität können jedoch auch die übrigen Rezepte dieses Buches für sich beanspruchen. Sie entstammen samt und sonders dem „Kiehnle Kochbuch", 1921 vom „schwäbischen Hausfrauenbund" im Hädecke-Verlag herausgebracht und seither in jedem ordentlichen schwäbischen Haushalt Garant für Originalität. Wenigstens in der Küche.

The original and authentic things of the past are becoming rarer and rarer. It's as if the characteristics that give a region its identity are disappearing one by one, pushed aside by the standardizing forces of globalization which seem to have reached even the furthest corners of the world. There are a few places that have been spared, by coincidence, and someday soon perhaps even these last bastions may be conquered by the likes of McDonalds and Co.

Yet, today more than ever, authenticity bears a stronger fascination than at any time in the past. People suffering from bouts of nostalgia and cravings for the food of their childhoods, are prepared to go miles out of their way simply to enjoy the taste of home-made food like "spätzle". A hundred years ago this would have been unthinkable – the only food that was available was prepared by hand.

Swabian *Spätzle* and Bavarian potato dumplings are probably the only dishes that have been able to defy this foreign influence, two remaining culinary bastions that continue to resist the fad of changing things for change's sake. The most frequent victim of this fad must be Swabian *Maultaschen* which are best described as a kind of giant ravioli. These days, you can even find them on the menus in the local village inns, filled with salmon rather than the original minced veal and spinach stuffing. Other traditional dishes disappeared long ago. One example is the *Beugel*, which vanished locally at the beginning of the last century never to be seen again, only to reappear unexpectedly in the New World in the form of the bagel – first in Toronto, then later in New York, where its popularity continues to this day.

Together with the *Fastenbretzel* (the Lent Pretzel), the Beugel was one of the most popular pastries eaten during Lent. Traditionally it was brought home from the local baker on the way back from confession at church, all as part of the purification ritual before Easter.

The *Beugel* was part of a traditional custom, and that perhaps is an explanation for its disappearance. As the traditional customs disappear, so do the foods that once accompanied them.

Some of the traditional foods cannot claim an exclusivity to their particular region that would qualify them as "truly original" since similar dishes can often be found across the regional borders; for example, *Bubaspitzle*, known in Frankonia as *Wargele* or *Bauchstecherle*; and *saure Rädle* known in Bavaria as *saures Kartoffelgmües*.

Even something as archetypically Swabian as *Gaisburger Marsch* – a traditional Swabian soup whose origins were documented by Thaddäus Troll (famous Swabian author), has an Austrian counterpart, which can be found in the historical records of military cuisine, the so called "Grenadier March" – the ingredients and preparation are identical in both recipes apart from the *Spätzle*. Austrian military cooks used pasta instead of *Spätzle* for this traditional Saturday meal, which really just used up the left-overs from the previous week, in particular any remaining beef.

There is no doubt that *Spätzle* will continue to hold its ground. As mentioned in the foreword of the first edition of this book, in the future, *Spätzle* will be, "the only product that Swabians of the 21st century will continue to prepare just as they did 700 years ago."

All the same, the remaining recipes in this book, can also claim to be authentic. They all come from the "Kiehnle Cookery Book" published by Hädecke in 1921, for the "Swabian Housewives Association", and have been a guarantee for authentic recipes in every proper Swabian household ever since.

Schupfnudeln · Rolled potato noodles

Schupfnudeln
(Bubespitzle, Wargele)

1 kg Kartoffeln am Tag zuvor gekocht
2–3 Eier, je 1 Prise Salz und Muskat
ca. 100 g Weizenmehl
4 l kochendes Salzwasser
Butterschmalz zum Braten

evtl. zum Aufziehen:
1–2 Eier
2–3 EL süße Sahne

Die Kartoffeln schälen, fein reiben, die Eier und
die Gewürze und soviel Mehl zufügen, bis die
Masse zusammenhält (das hängt von der Kartof-
felsorte ab). Den Teig durchkneten, eine Rolle formen, davon kleine Portionen abschneiden und mit
den Händen auf einem bemehlten Backbrett klein-
fingerlange Würstchen formen. Die Schupfnudeln
in leicht gesalzenem Wasser so lange kochen, bis
sie an die Oberfläche kommen. Eventuell erst eine
Probenudel abkochen, und wenn diese zerfällt,
noch etwas Mehl unterkneten.
Die Bubespitzle gut abtropfen lassen, sodann im
heißen Butterschmalz rundum knusprig braten
und zu Sauerkraut oder Braten reichen.
Oder die abgetropften Schupfnudeln auf einem
Backbrett ausbreiten, und wenn sie gut abgetropft
sind, in eine gefettete Form legen, mit verquirltem
Ei und Sahne übergießen und im vorgeheizten
Backofen bei ca. 200°C (Gasherd Stufe 3) etwa
20 Minuten goldgelb überbacken.
Das Hin-und-Her-Rollen der Kartoffelmasse nennt
man – je nach Gegend – schupfen oder wargeln.

Saure Kartoffelblättchen
(Kartoffelrädle)

1 kg festkochende Kartoffeln

zur Soße:
40 g Butter oder Pflanzenmargarine
60 g Mehl
$^3/_4$–1 l gut gewürzte Fleischbrühe
2–3 EL Weinessig
1 Lorbeerblatt
2 Nelken
$^1/_2$ Glas Weißwein

zum Nachwürzen:
Salz und frische Majoranblättchen

Die Kartoffeln schälen, in feine Scheiben schneiden und über Dampf knapp gar kochen. Das Wasser abgießen, die Kartoffeln in eine vorgewärmte
Schüssel füllen.
Butter oder Margarine zerlassen, das Mehl zugeben und unter Rühren eine braune Mehlschwitze
herstellen. Mit Fleischbrühe ablöschen, Essig und
Gewürze zugeben und die Soße 20 Minuten auf
kleiner Flamme köcheln.
Die Soße durch ein Sieb passieren, den Wein
unterrühren und die Soße nach Geschmack nachwürzen.
Die Karoffelblättchen einlegen, vorsichtig erhitzen
und servieren.

Oder den Majoran weglassen und das Kartoffelge-
richt mit 4 Esslöffeln, in Fleischbrühe gegarten
Zwiebelstücken und gehackter Petersilie würzen.

Die Kartoffelrädle können nur mit einem Kopfsalat
oder auch mit gekochtem Rindfleisch serviert werden.

---

*   Originalrezept aus „Oekonomisches Handbuch
     für Frauenzimmer", Stuttgart 1817.

Rolled potato noodles*

approx 2.2 lb potatoes, boiled the
    previous day
2–3 eggs
a pinch each of salt and nutmeg
approx 4 oz flour
approx 8 pt boiling salted water
lard for frying

Alternative serving possibility:

1–2 eggs
2–3 tbsp single cream

Peel the potatoes, grate finely. Add the eggs and
seasoning along with enough flour for the mixture
to stick together (the amount will depend on the
type of potato). Knead the dough thoroughly and
form a sausage shaped roll. Cut into slices. On a
floured board, roll each slice into a finger shaped
sausage. Boil in slightly salted water until they
float to the surface.
(It's a good idea to try one first – if it falls apart,
add a little more flour to the mixture.)
Drain well, and fry in hot butter until browned
and crisp. Serve with sauerkraut or pot-roast.
Alternatively, place the drained noodles in a
greased baking dish, pour over the beaten egg
and cream and bake in a preheated oven 390 °F
(gas mark 3) for about 20 minutes until golden
brown.
The rolling motion you use to form the potato
dough is known as *schupfen* or *wargeln* –
depending on the region.

Sour potato wheels

approx 2.2 lbs firm potatoes

For the sauce:

$1^1/_2$ oz butter or margarine
  2 oz flour
approx $1^1/_2$ pt well seasoned meat broth
2–3 tbsp wine vinegar
  1 bay leaf
  2 cloves
$^1/_2$ glass of white wine (Riesling or Kerner)

Additional seasoning:

salt and fresh marjoram leaves

Peel the potatoes and slice finely. Steam until
cooked through. Drain off excess water and place
the potatoes slices in a pre-heated dish.
Melt the butter or margarine, add the flour and
stir until you have a brown roux. De-glaze with
the meat broth. Then add the vinegar and the
seasoning. Simmer the sauce for 20 minutes at
low heat.
Run the sauce through a sieve, then add the wine
and season to taste.
Add the potato slices to the sauce and heat gently
before serving.

Alternatively:

Leave out the marjoram and season the potatoes
with 4 tablespoons of onion (cooked in the broth)
and chopped parsley.

The potato wheels can also be served simply with
a green salad or boiled beef.

---

* Original recipe from the old Swabian cookery book „Oeko-
    nomisches Handbuch für Frauenzimmer", Stuttgart 1817.

Linsen, Spätzle, Saiten
Lentils with Spätzle *and sausages*

Linsen, Spätzle, Saiten

Spätzle

Linsengemüse:
- 400 g Linsen, neue Ernte
- Wasser, 2 Lorbeerblätter
- 40 g geräucherter, durchwachsener Speck
- 50–60 g Mehl
- 1 Zwiebel
- 1 Gelbe Rübe, 1 Stück Lauch
- ca.$^1/_4$ l Fleischbrühe
- 2–3 EL Weinessig
- Salz und Pfeffer
- Spätzle, siehe nebenstehendes Rezept – halbe Menge
- Saiten vom Metzger, ersatzweise Wiener Würstchen

Die Linsen unter fließendem Wasser in einem Sieb überbrausen. Dann mit reichlich Wasser und den Lorbeerblättern aufsetzen und ca. 45 Minuten kochen – die Linsen sollten vom Kochwasser gut bedeckt sein.
Den Speck fein würfeln und auslassen. Darin das Mehl anrösten, bis es eine gelbbräunliche Farbe angenommen hat.
Die Zwiebel, Gelbe Rübe und den Lauch sehr fein hacken, kurz mit andünsten, dann die abgetropften Linsen zugeben und mit Fleischbrühe ablöschen. Mit Essig abschmecken und die Linsen gut durchkochen. Mit Salz und Pfeffer würzen.
Dazu gibt es Spätzle, Saiten oder ein gutes Rauchfleisch, das man auch kurze Zeit in den Linsen mitkochen kann.
Wer möchte, kann auch etwas frischen Knoblauch zu den kleingehackten Gemüsen geben – das macht das Gericht leichter verdaulich.Die Fleischbrühe kann auch durch einen Rotwein ersetzt werden – dann beim Abschmecken mit Essig vorsichtig sein.

Anmerkung: Ältere Linsen sollten über Nacht in viel Wasser eingeweicht und am nächsten Tag mit frischem Wasser gekocht werden. Keinesfalls Salz zugeben das verlängert die Kochzeit!

8 Portionen als Beilage:
- 500 g Weizenmehl
- 4–5 Eier
- 1 TL Salz
- $^1/_8$–$^1/_4$ l Wasser
- evtl.1 TL Öl für das Kochwasser
- heißes Wasser zum Schwenken

Das Mehl sieben, mit den Eiern und dem Salz in eine Schüssel geben. Unter Rühren nach und nach das Wasser zugeben und den Teig mit einem Kochlöffel (oder dem elektrischen Handrührgerät) so lange kräftig schlagen, bis kein Teigrest mehr am Löffel hängenbleibt, wenn er zur Probe in die Höhe gehalten wird. Den Teig für kurze Zeit ruhen lassen, dann nochmals gut durcharbeiten.
Ein Spätzlesbrett, dieses Brett ist nach vorne etwas abgeschrägt, mit Wasser benetzen, eine kleine Menge Teig daraufstreichen und mit einem breiten Messer oder Schaber dünne Teigstreifen in das schwach sprudelnde Kochwasser schaben. Während des Schabens das Brett und das Messer immer wieder in das sprudelnde Wasser tauchen das erleichtert die Arbeit! Schwimmen die Spätzle an der Oberfläche, mit einem Schaumlöffel herausnehmen und kurz im heißen Wasser schwenken, dann kleben die Spätzle hinterher nicht zusammen. Die fertigen Spätzle gut abtropfen lassen, auf eine vorgewärmte Platte legen und rasch servieren.
Die fertigen Spätzle können mit Butter, leicht gerösteten Semmelbröseln oder fein geschnittenen, braun gebratenen Zwiebelringen oder Speckwürfeln überschmälzt werden.
Früher wurde in manchen Familien Molke zum Anrühren des Teiges verwendet. Die Molke ist eigentlich ein Abfallprodukt, das beim Herstellen von Quark und Käse anfällt. Durch die Molke bekamen die Spätzle eine lockere Struktur.

Lentils with Spätzle and sausages

Lentils:
  14 oz lentils, new harvest
water, 2 bay leaves
$1^1/_2$ oz smoked lean bacon
approx 2 oz flour
  1 onion
  1 carrot, 1 piece of leek
approx 1 pt of meat stock
2–3 tbsp wine vinegar
salt and pepper
Spätzle, see next recipe – half quantity
  4 pairs of sausages from the butchers,
    alternatively Wiener sausages

Place the lentils in a sieve and rinse under running water. Place them in a pan with plenty of water and a bay leaf and boil for 45 minutes – the lentils should be well covered with water.
Dice the bacon and fry in a pan. Add the flour and fry until browned. Finely chop the onion, carrot and leek, and cook with the flour and bacon. Add the drained lentils and de-glaze with the meat stock. Season with vinegar to taste and cook thoroughly. Season with salt and pepper.

Serve with Spätzle, sausages or good smoked bacon (you can cook them briefly with the lentils). If you like, you can add some fresh garlic to the finely chopped vegetables – it makes the dish easier to digest. You can replace the meat stock with red wine – but be careful when adding the vinegar.

Comment: Older lentils should be left to soak over-night in plenty of water. Cook the following day in fresh water. Do not add salt – it will prolong the cooking time!

Spätzle

makes 8 side servings:
  1 lb wheat flour
4–5 eggs
  1 tsp salt
$^1/_4$–$^1/_2$ pt of water
  1 tsp oil for the water
extra hot water to rinse the noodles

Sieve the flour into a bowl. Add the eggs and the salt. Add the water bit by bit and beat the mixture until smooth. Using a wooden spoon (or electric mixer), knead the dough until nothing remains hanging on the spoon if you hold it up in the air. Leave the dough to rest and then knead again until it forms bubbles of air.
A *Spätzle* board, is a special board that has one side thinner than the other (but a normal chopping board will do – if it's not too heavy!). Sprinkle water over the surface and spread a small amount of dough on it (maximum ½ cm). Holding the board over the pan of simmering water, scrape off thin slices of the dough using a wide bladed knife or spatular. Once you have finished the first batch of dough, dip the board and the blade of the knife into the boiling hot water, it will stop the dough from sticking to the board and make the job easier!
Once the noodles rise to the surface they are done. Skim them off using a slotted spoon and rinse them quickly in hot water to prevent them from sticking together.
Drain the cooked noodles thoroughly and serve straight away in a pre-heated dish.

The finished noodles can be served with butter, lightly browned bread crumbs, finely sliced fried onion rings or bacon bits.
In the past, some families used whey to make the dough. Whey is actually a waste product left over from making curd and cheese, but it gave the noodles a lighter structure.

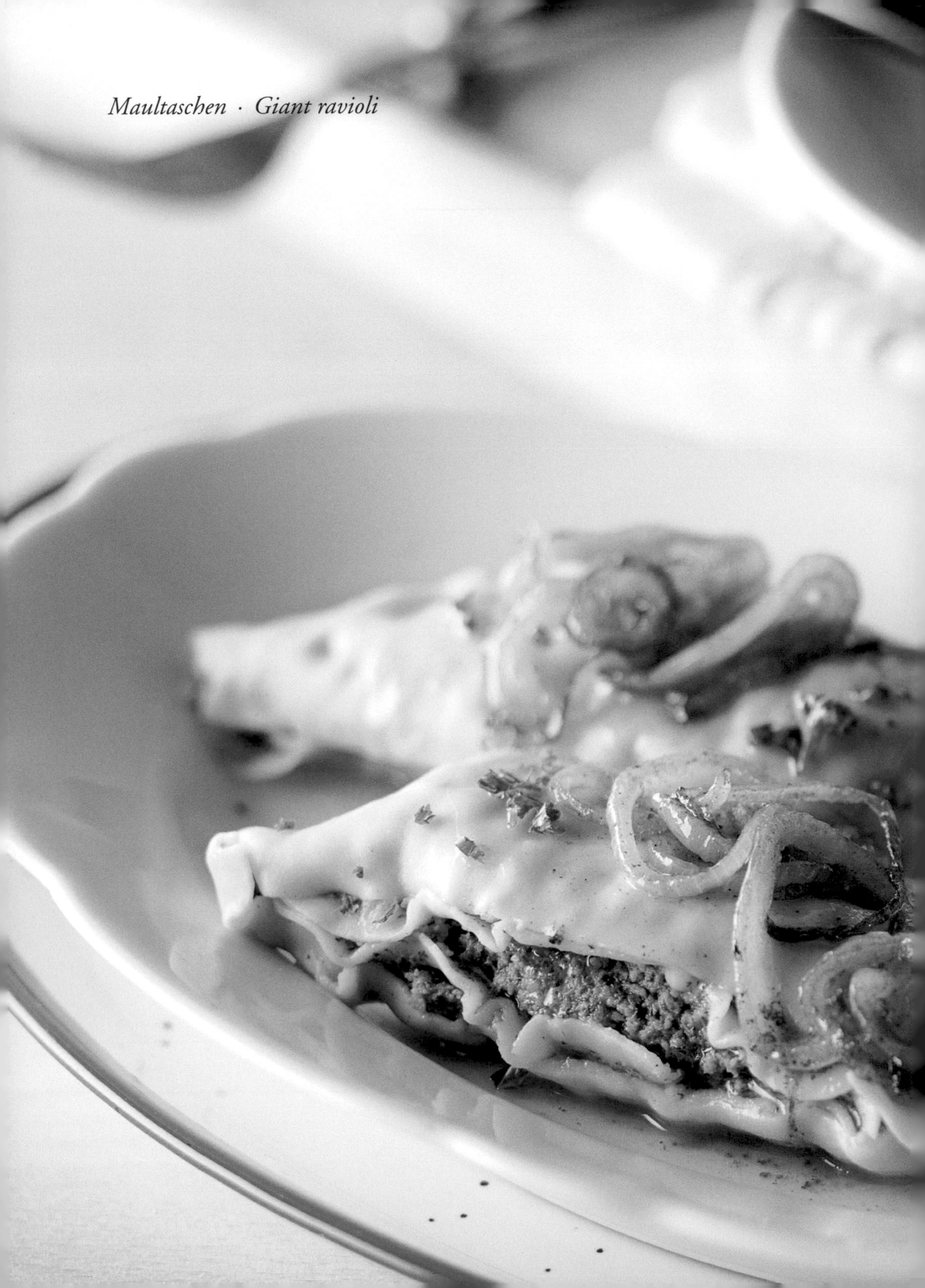

Maultaschen · Giant ravioli

Maultaschen

Nudelteig:
   3 Eier, etwas Salz
je Ei eine halbe Eischale Wasser
360–400 g Weizenmehl

Die Eier mit etwas Salz und dem Wasser verquirlen. Das Mehl in eine Schüssel sieben, in der Mitte eine Vertiefung formen und die Eier hineingießen. Alle Zutaten von der Mitte her vermischen, aus der Schüssel nehmen und den Teig auf dem Backbrett so lange kneten, bis er beim Durchschneiden kleine Löchlein zeigt. (Der Teig kann auch in der Küchenmaschine geknetet werden.)
Je nach Beschaffenheit des Mehles evtl. noch etwas Wasser oder ein Eiweiß unterkneten. Der Teig darf jedoch nicht zu weich sein. Eine Kugel formen und mit einer erwärmten Schüssel bedecken und ruhen lassen, währenddessen die *Füllung* zubereiten:

400 g frischer Spinat
Salzwasser
   20 g Speckwürfel
   20 g Butter
    1 kleine Zwiebel, fein gehackt
    1 Bund Petersilie, fein gehackt
3–4 trockene Brötchen, Rinde abgerieben
150 g gekochter Schinken oder kalter Braten,
      würfelig geschnitten
250 g Bratwurstbrät oder Hackfleisch
2–3 Eier
je 1 Prise Salz, Pfeffer und Muskat
kochendes Salzwasser oder Fleischbrühe

Den Spinat gut putzen, waschen und in kochendem Salzwasser kurz blanchieren. Kalt abschrecken, abtropfen lassen und nicht zu fein hacken. Die Speckwürfel in Butter anschwitzen, Zwiebelwürfelchen und Petersilie mitdünsten und abkühlen lassen. Die altbackenen Brötchen einweichen, gut ausdrücken und zerpflücken. In einer großen Schüssel diese Zutaten mit dem Schinken und dem Brät vermischen, die Eier unterarbeiten und mit Salz, Pfeffer und Muskat würzen. (Wenn Hackfleisch verwendet wird, so sollte dieses mit den Speck- und Zwiebelwürfelchen so lange gedünstet werden, bis es eine graue Farbe hat.)
Den Nudelteig portionsweise auf einer bemehlten Unterlage auswellen (ausrollen) entweder in längliche, etwa 20 cm breite Streifen oder in runde Nudelflecke schneiden. Die Füllung gleichmäßig auf eine Hälfte der Teigstreifen streichen oder kleine Häufchen aufsetzen, die unbestrichene Teighälfte darüberklappen, den Teig gut andrücken und so verfahren, bis alles verbraucht ist.
Nun nicht zu große Recht- oder Vierecke davon abrädeln, in strudelndes Salzwasser oder Fleischbrühe einlegen und je nach Größe ca. 10 bis 15 Minuten darin ziehen, nicht kochen, lassen.
Die fertigen Maultaschen können in der Brühe mit gerösteten Semmelbröseln und Petersilie oder mit Zwiebelringen serviert werden: 20 g Butter zerlassen, 2 Esslöffel feine Semmelbrösel darin leicht anrösten sowie einen Bund Petersilie klein hacken und darüber anrichten.
Oder eine in feine Ringe geschnittene Zwiebel in Butter braun braten und über die Maultaschen geben. Dazu schmeckt ein „schlonziger" Kartoffelsalat, das ist ein relativ nasser Kartoffelsalat, angemacht mit fein gehackter Zwiebel, Salz, Pfeffer, guter Fleischbrühe und vielleicht auch etwas Kochwasser von den Maultaschen, Essig und Sonnenblumenöl, Rezept Seite 48.
Übrig gebliebene Maultaschen können am nächsten Tag, in daumendicke Streifen geschnitten, in Fett angebraten werden. Eier mit etwas Milch verrühren, darübergießen und stocken lassen. Mit gehackter Petersilie bestreuen. Dazu schmeckt grüner Salat oder Kartoffelsalat, vermischt mit Endivienstreifen.

Giant ravioli

Noodle dough:

   3 eggs, a pinch of salt
half an eggshell full of water for each egg
12$^1/_2$ oz   flour

Mix the eggs with the salt and the water. Sieve the flour into a bowl, form a hollow in the middle and pour in the eggs. Mix all the ingredients together, working from the middle. Remove the dough from the bowl and knead on a board until small bubbles begin to form in the dough (you can also knead the dough with an electric mixer). Depending on the sort of flour you use, you may need to add a little more water or an extra egg-white to the dough, but it should not be too soft. Shape the dough into a ball, cover with a bowl and leave to rest. In the meantime you can begin preparing the filling:

   14 oz fresh spinach
salt water
   $^3/_4$ oz bacon bits
   $^3/_4$ oz butter
   1 small onion, finely chopped
   1 bunch of parsley, finely chopped
3–4 dry bread rolls with the crusts scraped off
   5 oz boiled ham or cold roast meat
8$^1/_2$ oz sausage meat or minced meat
2–3 eggs
a pinch of salt, pepper and nutmeg
boiling salt water or meat stock

Sort and clean the spinach thoroughly and blanche in boiling salt water. Rinse in cold water, drain and chop (not too finely).
Braise the bacon bits in butter, add the onions and parsley and then leave to cool. Soak the old rolls in water. Squeeze them out and tear them into small pieces. In a large bowl, mix these ingredients with the ham and the roasted meat, add the eggs and season with salt, pepper and nutmeg. (If you use minced beef, you will need to fry it with the bacon bits and onions until the meat turns grey in colour).

Roll out portions of the dough on a floured surface to a thickness of 2 mm, as big as possible, either in long strips, approx 20 cm wide, or in circles (approx 10 cm diameter). Spread one half of each dough strip with some of the filling, or place small heaps on the circles of dough. Fold the other half of the dough strip over the filling to form rectangles, or semi-circles if you are chose the round shape, and seal the edges well. Continue until you have used up all the mixture.

Using a pasta cutting wheel, slice the filled dough into squares or rectangles. Simmer in hot salt water or broth for between 10 or 15 minutes. Do not allow them to boil.

The finished *Maultaschen* can be served in the meat stock with fried breadcrumbs and parsley or with onion rings:

Melt ¾ ounces of butter. Fry two tablespoons of breadcrumbs in the butter, then add a small bunch of finely chopped parsley. Sprinkle these over the *Maultaschen* and serve.

Alternatively, fry the finely sliced onion rings in butter until brown and pour them over the *Maultaschen*. This tastes good served with sloppy (*schlonziger*) Swabian potato salad, which is fairly moist, and garnished with finely chopped onions, salt, pepper, good meat stock and perhaps a little of the water that was used to boil the *Maultaschen*, as well as vinegar and sunflower oil (recipe on page 49).

Left-over Maultaschen can be eaten the following day. Cut into finger thick slices and fry in oil. Mix the eggs with a little milk, pour over the fried *Maultaschen* and allow to set. Sprinkle with chopped parsley. This tastes good served with a green salad or a potato salad mixed with endive strips.

Schwäbischer Rostbraten
Swabian rump steak

Schwäbischer Rostbraten

4 Scheiben Rostbraten je ca. 180–200 g
Salz und frisch gemahlener Pfeffer
zerlassene Butter oder gutes Speiseöl
4 mittelgroße Zwiebeln
Butterschmalz zum Braten
1 Schuss Rotwein
4 EL süße Sahne

Die Fleischscheiben leicht klopfen und den Rand
mehrmals einkerben (damit sich das Fleisch beim
Braten nicht hochwölbt). Mit Salz und Pfeffer
sparsam würzen und mit etwas Butter oder Öl be-
pinseln. Auf den heißen Rost – wie in alten Rezep-
ten – legen und rasch von beiden Seiten anbraten.
Je nach Geschmack den Rostbraten „englisch"
oder durchbraten. Fühlt sich das Fleisch beim
Druck mit der Fingerspitze elastisch an, so ist es
innen noch blutig. Je fester es sich anfühlt, desto
durchgebratener ist es.
Die Zwiebeln in feine Ringe schneiden und im heißen Bratfett in der Pfanne schön kross braten.
Über den Rostbraten anrichten. Es empfiehlt sich
in jedem Falle, die Zwiebeln separat zu braten.
Man kann den Rostbraten auch in einer schweren
(schmiede- oder gusseisernen) Pfanne zubereiten:
Die vorbereiteten Fleischscheiben im heißen
Butterschmalz rasch von beiden Seiten anbraten,
dann pro Seite noch 3 bis 4 Minuten weiter-
braten. Mit Salz und Pfeffer würzen, aus der
Pfanne nehmen und auf einer Platte bedeckt
warm halten.
Den Bratfond mit wenig Rotwein aufkochen, kurz
einkochen und die Sahne unterrühren, abschmecken. Dieses kurze Sößle zu dem Rostbraten servieren.
Rostbraten kann mit Bauernbrot oder mit Sauerkraut und Spätzle oder nur mit Spätzle und Salat
serviert werden.

Gefüllte Kalbsbrust

1,5 kg Kalbsbrust, vom Metzger ausgelöst
und vorbereitet
250 g Kalbsknochen klein gehackt
80 g Butter (zerlassen)
1 Zwiebel, 1 gelbe Rübe
Salz, Pfeffer

für die Fülle:
3 alte Semmeln
$1/2$ mittelgroße Zwiebel, fein geschnitten
40 g Butter, Petersilie
2 Eier, $1/8$ l Milch
fein abgeriebene Schale von einer
ungespritzten Zitrone
Muskatnuss, Salz

Die Kalbsbrust innen und außen gut mit Salz und
Pfeffer einreiben. Die Semmeln klein schneiden
und mit der in Butter angeschwitzten Zwiebel, der
klein gehackten Petersilie, den in Milch verquirlten
Eiern und Zitronenschale sowie den Gewürzen gut
vermengen und eine Viertelstunde ruhen lassen.
Die Masse nicht zu fest in die Brusttasche füllen
und die Brust zunähen.
Die Kalbsknochen in einen Bräter geben, die Brust
mit der Oberseite nach unten darauf legen, mit
der zerlassenen Butter bestreichen und bei starker
Hitze (ca. 250 °C) im Backofen kräftig anbraten.
Die Hitze nach einer Viertelstunde reduzieren, die
geviertelte Zwiebel und in Scheiben geschnittene
gelbe Rübe zugeben und seitlich etwas Wasser
angießen. Nach einer halben Stunde die Brust um-
drehen und unter ständigem Begießen (da sonst
die Brust austrocknet) eine weitere Stunde fertig
braten. Darauf achten, dass die Kalbsbrust nicht
zu dunkelbraun wird. Vor dem Anschneiden eine
halbe Stunde im ausgeschalteten, geöffneten
Backrohr ruhen lassen.
Zur Kalbsbrust isst man am besten Kartoffelsalat.

Swabian rump steak

4 slices of rump steak, each approx 6–7 oz
salt and freshly milled pepper
melted butter or a good quality oil
4 medium sized onions
clarified butter for frying
a dash of red wine
4 tbsp single cream

Pound the slices of meat a little and nick the edges so that the meat does not curl up when fried. Season sparingly with salt and pepper and brush with a little oil. Place on a griddle and roast quickly on both sides until rare or well done – whatever you prefer. If the meat feels soft when you prod it with your finger, then it is still rare. The harder it feels, the more cooked through it is. Cut the onions into fine rings and fry in the pan until nice and crisp. Arrange the onion rings on the steaks and serve.
It is better to fry the onions separately from the meat, otherwise they will turn soggy.
The meat can also be prepared in a heavy cast iron pan or skillet.
As above, pound the meat and nick the edges. Fry the meat in hot clarified butter on both sides, and then fry for a further 3–4 minutes. Season with salt and pepper and remove from the pan. Cover the meat and keep it warm.
De-glaze the pan with red wine and reduce the sauce. Stir in the cream and season to taste. Serve the sauce with the meat.

Swabian rump steaks can be served with country bread, or sauerkraut and *Spätzle*, or simply with *Spätzle* and salad.

Stuffed breast of veal

3 lb breast of veal, deboned and prepared
    by your butcher
8$\frac{1}{2}$ oz finely chopped veal bones
3 oz butter (melted)
1 onion
1 carrot
salt and pepper

For the filling:
3 old bread rolls
$\frac{1}{2}$ medium sized onion, finely chopped
1$\frac{1}{2}$ oz butter
2 tbsp parsley, finely chopped
2 eggs, $\frac{1}{4}$ pt milk
finely grated rind of $\frac{1}{2}$ unwaxed lemon
nutmeg, salt

Preheat the oven to 450°F.
Rub the inside of the meat with salt and pepper. Fry the onions in the butter until translucent. Mix the eggs, milk, lemon rind and seasoning. Cut the bread rolls into small pieces and mix with the onions, finely chopped parsley, and the egg mix. Leave to rest for quarter of an hour.
Stuff the breast of veal with the mixture, but do not overfill. Sew the meat closed.
Put the veal bones in the roasting dish and place the breast of veal (facedown) on top. Brush with the melted butter and roast in the preheated oven (approx 480°F). After 15 minutes, reduce the heat and add the quartered onion and the sliced carrots. Pour a little water into the side of the pan.
After half an hour, turn the meat over, continue to roast for a further hour. Baste the meat regularly (every 15 minutes) to prevent it from drying out. Make sure that the meat does not turn too brown. Turn off the oven and open the oven door. Leave the meat to rest in the oven for 30 minutes before carving it.
Best served with potato salad.

Metzelsupp · Butcher's broth

Metzelsupp

Eine gute Metzelsupp kann die Lebensgeister wieder aufrichten – schon der Dichter Ludwig Uhland wusste dies und widmete deshalb ein Gedicht dieser einfachen, aber guten Speise! Die Metzelsupp ist eigentlich ein „Abfallprodukt", das beim Schlachten anfällt. Die Voraussetzung für eine gute Metzelsupp ist einmal, dass frisch geschlachtet wird, und zum anderen, dass ein paar Blut- und Leberwürste „aus Versehen" platzen, damit die Suppe nicht gar zu dünn ist!

Einen großen Wurstkessel (etwa so groß, wie früher die Waschkessel waren) zur Hälfte mit Wasser füllen und zum Kochen bringen. Da hinein kommen nacheinander Knochen (es darf noch Fleisch dran sein!), Speck, Fleisch und Schwarten etc. Kleinere Stücke in ein Netz einlegen, man kann sie später besser herausfischen. Dazu kommt Suppengrün ebenfalls in einem Netz –, und zwar

4–5 Stangen Lauch (Porree)
500 g Gelbe Rüben
1 Sellerieknolle
2–3 Petersilienwurzeln
1 kg Zwiebeln

alles grob zerschnitten. Dieses Gemüse gart etwa eine Stunde mit. Die Zwiebeln können anschließend zur Wurstherstellung verwendet werden.

In die Brühe kommen dann die Kochwürste wie Leberwurst, Blutwurst. Dabei darauf achten, dass die Temperatur im Wurstkessel 80 °C nicht überschreitet (evtl. etwas kaltes Wasser zufügen), die Würste platzen sonst! Während des Garens die Würste immer wieder unter die Oberfläche drücken und eventuell mit einer Stopfnadel einige Male einstechen, damit sich die Einlage gleichmäßig verteilt. Die Würste

sind nach ca. 1 bis 2 Stunden gar – je nach Dicke. Die Menge Metzelsupp, die serviert werden soll, aus dem Wurstkessel entnehmen und eventuell noch einmal mit Suppengrün und Lorbeerblatt ca. 30 Minuten kochen. Dann das Gemüse entfernen, die Suppe mit Salz, Pfeffer und Majoran abschmecken und in Teller füllen. Schwarzbrotwürfelchen in Schweineschmalz anrösten und zusammen mit frischen Schnittlauchröllchen über der Metzelsupp anrichten. Dazu schmeckt ein frisches Holzofenbrot.

So säumet denn, ihr Freunde, nicht, die Würste zu verspeisen, und lasst zum würzigen Gericht die Becher fleißig kreisen! Es reimt sich trefflich Wein und Schwein, und passt sich köstlich Wurst und Durst; bei Würsten gilt's zu bürsten.

Auch unser edles Sauerkraut, wir sollen's nicht vergessen; ein Deutscher hat's zuerst gebaut, drum ist's ein deutsches Essen. Wenn solch ein Fleischchen weiß und mild im Kraute liegt, das ist ein Bild wie Venus in den Rosen.

Und wird von schönen Händen dann das schöne Fleisch zerleget, das ist, was einem deutschen Mann gar süß das Herz beweget. Gott Amor naht und lächelt still und denkt: „Nur daß, wer küssen will, zuvor den Mund sich wische!"

Ihr Freunde, tadle keiner mich, dass ich von Schweinen singe! Es knüpfen Kraftgedanken sich oft an geringe Dinge. Ihr kennt jenes alte Wort, ihr wisst. Es findet hier und dort ein Schwein auch ein Perle.

Aus dem „Metzelsuppenlied"
von Ludwig Uhland

Butcher's broth

According to the poet Ludwig Uhland, a good Metzel soup can bring the dead back to life, and that's why he dedicated a poem to this simple, but good meal!

Butcher's broth is actually made from the leftovers at slaughtering time. For a good Butcher's broth, it is important that the leftovers are fresh, and that one or two of the liver and blood sausages in the soup "accidently" burst, so that the soup is not too thin!

Half-fill a large sausage pan (about as big as wash tubs used to be) with water and bring it to the boil. Then one at a time add the bones (they can still have some meat on them!), bacon, meat and rinds etc. Place any smaller bits in a piece of muslin so that they are easy to take out later, along with a second piece of muslin cloth filled with the following:

4–5 leeks
1 lb carrots
    1 celleriac bulb
2–3 parsely roots
approx 2.2 lb onions

Roughly chop all the vegetables, cook them in the soup for about an hour. They can be used later to make sausages.

Then add the sausages – you can use freshly made, uncooked liver sausage (page 37), black pudding (page 41). Please be careful that the temperature of the pan does not exceed 175°F (if necessary add cold water), otherwise the sausages will burst!

While they are cooking, repeatedly push the sausages under the surface and if necessary prick them with a darning needle, so that the sausage meat is cooked evenly.

The sausages will be done after one to two hours – depending on how thick they are.

Take the amount of soup to be served from the large pan and cook for a further half an hour in a smaller pan together with some mixed greens and a bay leaf.

Remove the vegetables, season the soup with salt, pepper and marjoram, then ladle into soup bowls. Roast some black bread croutons in pork dripping, and sprinkle over the soup with some freshly chopped chives.

This tastes good serves with country bread baked in a wood fired oven.

One of the most popular poems by Ludwig Uhland, the famous 19th century Swabian poet, whose 200th birthday was celebrated 1987, is the Metzelsuppenlied, the "Song about the Butcher's Broth".

In his poem, Uhland not only makes clear that swine rhymes with wine, and wurst with thirst, but elevates the profane event further, in the lines

Wenn solch ein Fleischchen weiß und mild
im Kraute liegt, das ist ein Bild
wie Venus in den Rosen.

Here he compares a slab of pork laying on a bed of Sauerkraut with "Venus in den Rosen". This "Venus in the roses" refers to a turn of phrase used by Minnesänger, the troubadours of the Middle Ages.

By making this comparison, Uhland ran a risk of upsetting people, with these two contrasting images. We can tell that he was aware of this, because in the lines that follow in his last verse, he says

Pray, my friend, don't scold me now
When of pigs I sing;
There have at times been stronger thoughts
Tied to a lesser thing
And, without doubt, you are aware
That on occasion here and there
Even a swine may find a pearl.

Sauerkraut mit Kesselfleisch und
Leber-/Griebenwurst

Sauerkraut with boiled pork,
liver sausage and black pudding

Sauerkraut mit Kesselfleisch und Leber-/Griebenwurst

Leberwürste

500 g Schweinebauch, -bug oder -hals, auch
halbierter Schweinskopf oder Häxle
1/2 l Fleischbrühe
1 Zwiebel, grob zerschnitten
1 kg frisches Sauerkraut (z. B. Filderkraut)
50–60 g Schweineschmalz
evtl. einige Schinkenabschnitte
1 große Zwiebel, fein geschnitten
1 Kartoffel
Wacholderbeeren oder Kümmel
2–3 Lorbeerblätter
Apfelsaft oder Weißwein zum Angießen
Griebenwurst, siehe Seite 40

750 g durchwachsenes Schweinefleisch
250 g fetter, ungeräucherter Speck
1 1/2–2 l Wasser, 1 EL Salz
1 Spickzwiebel (mit 4 Nelken)
2 Lorbeerblätter
einige Pfefferkörner, zerdrückt
500 g frische Schweineleber
1 geriebene Zwiebel
Salz und frisch gemahlener Pfeffer
1 TL gerebelter Majoran
je 1/2 TL Piment und Thymian gemahlen
gereinigte Schweinedärme

Das Fleisch waschen, in daumendicke Scheiben schneiden, in die mit Zwiebelstücken angereicherte Brühe einlegen und ca. 40–50 Minuten sanft kochen. Das Fleisch aus der Brühe nehmen, einen Viertelliter der Brühe für das Kraut weiterverwenden.
Das Sauerkraut etwas kürzer schneiden. In einem innen emaillierten Topf das Schmalz zerlassen, Schinkenstückchen oder Speckwürfel und Zwiebelwürfel darin glasig werden lassen. Das Kraut zugeben, kurz anschwitzen und mit Fleischbrühe angießen. Die Kartoffel schälen, fein reiben und unter das Kraut mischen. Je nach Geschmack Wacholderbeeren und Lorbeerblätter oder nur Kümmel zugeben. Die Fleischscheiben auf das Kraut legen, den Deckel schließen und das Kraut auf kleiner Flamme ca. 2 bis 3 Stunden kochen. In regelmäßigen Abständen das Kraut etwas auflockern, Apfelsaft oder Weißwein zugießen – Kerner eignet sich gut, aber auch ein Riesling ist empfehlenswert.
Wird das Kraut ohne Kesselfleisch gekocht, zur Geschmacksabrundung einen Apfel in Stückchen unter das Kraut mischen.
Kesselfleisch mit Senf und Pfeffer servieren.

Das Schweinefleisch etwa 45 Minuten, und in den letzten 20 Minuten den Speck zusammen in dem mit Spickzwiebel und Gewürzen versehenen Salzwasser kochen. Die Leber häuten, putzen (Adern entfernen) und in Scheiben schneiden. In ein Sieb legen und einige Male in die kochende Brühe eintauchen, insgesamt etwa 3 bis 4 Minuten.
Das Fleisch und die Leber durch den Fleischwolf (feine Scheibe) drehen, den Speck sehr klein würfeln. Alle Zutaten in eine Schüssel geben und soviel durchgesiebte Kochbrühe zugeben, bis eine dickflüssige Masse entsteht. Sollte die Masse zu dünn geraten, so können 2 bis 3 altbackene Brötchen (die Kruste abreiben, Brötchen in feine Scheiben schneiden, kurz mit heißem Wasser befeuchten und ausdrücken, dann zerrupfen) untergemengt werden. Die geriebene Zwiebel und die Gewürze zufügen, gut abschmecken. Die Wurstmasse in gut gereinigte Därme (kann man im Fleischereibedarfsgeschäft bekommen) drei Viertel hoch einfüllen und die Würste abbinden. Mit einer Stopfnadel mehrmals einstechen und in leicht gesalzenem Wasser oder in der Metzelsupp (siehe S. 32) bei 80°C in ca. 30 bis 45 Minuten garen.

Sauerkraut with boiled pork, liver sausage & black pudding

Liver sausages

1 lb pork belly, shoulder, neck, and half a pig's
    head or knuckle
1 pt meat stock
1 onion, roughly chopped
approx 2.2 lb fresh Sauerkraut
$1^{1}/_{2}$–2 oz pork lard
if you have them, some left-over bits of ham
    1 large onion, finely chopped
    1 potato
juniper berries or caraway
2–3 bay leaves
apple juice or white wine
black pudding, see page 41

$1^{1}/_{2}$ lb marbled pork
$8^{1}/_{2}$ oz fatty unsmoked bacon
3–4 pt water
    1 tbsp salt
    1 onion larded with 4 cloves
    2 bay leaves
a few peppercorns, ground
    1 lb fresh pork liver
    1 grated onion
salt and freshly milled pepper
    1 tsp ground marjoram
    $^{1}/_{2}$ tsp of ground pimento and $^{1}/_{2}$ tsp ground
    thyme
cleaned sausage casings (pig intestines)

Wash the meat and cut it into slices as thick as your thumb. Place in the meat stock with the roughly cut onions, and simmer gently for 40–50 minutes. Remove the meat from the stock and use ½ pint of the stock for the cabbage.

Cut the sauerkraut into shorter strips. Melt the lard in an enamel saucepan then add the bits of ham or bacon together with the diced onions and fry until they are translucent. Add the cabbage. Allow it to sweat for a moment and then pour in the meat stock. Peel the potato, grate it finely and stir it into the cabbage. Depending on what you prefer, season with juniper berries and bay leaves, or just the caraway seeds. Place the meat on top of the cabbage, seal the pan with a closely fitting lid and leave to cook over a low heat for 2 to 3 hours.

Use a spoon to loosen up the cabbage at regular intervals adding apple juice or white wine – Kerner is good, but a Riesling is also ideal. If you choose to cook the cabbage without meat, then add some apple slices to the cabbage and stir them in.

Serve the meat with mustard and pepper.

Cook the pork for about 25 minutes in the salt water together with the spices. Add the bacon and cook for a further 20 minutes.

Skin the liver, clean it and remove any veins, then cut it into slices. Place in a sieve and dip into the boiling broth a few times, so that it is in the water for a total of about 3–4 minutes.

Run the meat and the liver through a mincer (use the fine blade), and dice the bacon very finely. Place all the ingredients in a bowl and add enough of the sieved broth to make a thick paste. If the mixture becomes too thin, you can add 2 or 3 old bread rolls to the mix. (Remove the crusts first, then slice them into pieces. Quickly soak them in hot water, squeeze them out straight away and tear them into bits).

Add the grated onion and season well. Clean the sausage casings thoroughly, (you can get them at a good butcher's shop). Fill them three quarters full with the sausage meat and tie them closed. Using a darning needle, pierce them a few times, cook them in lightly salted water, or in Butcher's Broth (see page 33) at 175 °F for between 30 to 45 minutes.

Flädlesuppe · Beef broth with shredded pancakes

Griebenwurst

Flädlesuppe

Für etwa 10 kg Wurst:
  2 kg Schweineschwarten mit Speckschicht
  5 kg Schweinebacken und Rüssel, evtl. vor-
    gepökelt
reichlich Kochwasser, evtl. Salz
  1 kg frische Schweineleber
  1 kg Schweineblut
evtl. Antigerinnungsmittel für das Blut
  1 kg Brühe

pro Kilo Wurstmasse:
 18 g Salz, wenn das Fleisch nicht gepökelt
     war
3–5 g schwarzer Pfeffer, gemahlen
  5 g Piment, gemahlen
5–8 g Majoranpulver
gut gereinigte Schweinedärme

Die Schwarten ca. 1½ Stunden, Schweinebacken und Rüssel ca. 1 Stunde in Wasser (falls vorgepökelt, kein Salz zugeben) kochen. Das Fleisch sollte auf Daumendruck elastisch nachgeben. Die Leber nur 30 Minuten mitkochen. Die Schwarten im Blitzhacker zu einem feinen Brei verarbeiten (die Masse sollte wie Pudding sein), Schweinebacken und Rüssel durch die feine Scheibe des Fleischwolfs treiben. Die Leber in sehr kleine Würfel schneiden. Den Schwartenbrei auf genau 40 °C erhitzen, das gut gerührte Blut zugeben (will man sicher gehen, dass es nicht gerinnt, ein entsprechendes Mittel zusetzen), den Fleischbrei und die Brühe sowie die Leberstückchen unterarbeiten. Mit den Gewürzen gut abschmecken und die Masse in gereinigte Därme nicht zu prall einfüllen. Die Würste abbinden und evtl. stupfen (siehe auch S. 36). Im 75–80 °C heißen Wasser ca. 45 Minuten kochen. Danach kurz in kaltes Wasser tauchen, damit der Darm nicht hart wird, und frisch zu Sauerkraut servieren.

150 g Weizenmehl
knapp ¼ l Milch
1–2 Eier
  1 Prise Salz

zum Ausreiben der Pfanne:
  1 Stück Speck oder Speckschwarte

außerdem:
  1 l gute Fleischbrühe
  1 Bund Schnittlauch

Aus Mehl, Milch, den Eiern und der Prise Salz einen glatten, nicht zu dicken Teig rühren. Eine schwere Bratpfanne stark erhitzen, mit Speck ausreiben, einen kleinen Schöpflöffel Teig hineingeben, verlaufen lassen und dünne Pfannküchle – Flädle – backen. So verfahren, bis der ganze Teig verbraucht ist. Die Flädle abkühlen lassen, halbieren und in dünne Streifen schneiden. In klare, sehr heiße Fleischbrühe einlegen und sofort servieren. Mit Schnittlauchröllchen bestreuen.

Flädle sind ein Bestandteil der bekannten „Schwäbischen Hochzeitssuppe". Je nach Landstrich kommen noch Grießklöße, Markklöße und Brätklöße oder Leberklöße, kleine Maultäschle oder Backerbsle, Eierstich und Leberknöpfle mit in die gute Suppe. Da in früheren Zeiten Vorschriften des Landesvaters auch Tauf- oder Hochzeitsessen reglementierten, fielen die einzelnen Gänge eben besonders reichhaltig aus – so wurden die Vorschriften zu Gunsten des Essers ausgelegt!

Black Pudding (blood sausage)

for approx 22 lb of sausages:
 4½ lb pork rinds with a layer of bacon on
   them
 11 lb pig cheeks and snout,
   (already salted is fine)
plenty of water for boiling – salt, if required
approx 2.2 lb fresh pork liver
approx 2.2 lb pig's blood
optional: anti-coagulant for the blood
approx 2.2 lb stock

per 2.2 lb of sausage meat:
 ¾ oz salt, if the meat was not already salted
 ¾ tsp black pepper, ground
 1 tsp allspice (pimento), ground
 1½ tsp marjoram powder
well-cleaned sausage casings

Cook the pork rinds for about 1½ hours. The pig's cheeks and snout only need to be cooked for 1 hour (if they were already salted do not add extra salt to the water). The liver only needs to cook for 30 minutes. Using a kitchen machine (rough blade), mince the rinds until they are the consistency of thick custard. Using the fine blade, work the pig's cheeks and snout through the machine, then cut the liver into very small cubes. Heat the minced rinds to exactly 105 °F, add the well stirred blood (if you want to ensure that the blood does not coagulate, use an anti-coagulant), the mince mixture and the stock, as well as the diced liver. Mix well. Season well with the spices and fill the sausage casings, but do not overfill. Tie the sausages closed and puncture with a needle, so that the sausage meat cooks evenly. Cook in hot water at 165–175 °F for 45 minutes. Then plunge them in cold water, to prevent the skins from hardening, then serve with sauerkraut.

Beef broth with shredded pancakes

 5 oz flour
just under ½ cup milk
1–2 eggs
a pinch of salt

For greasing the pan:
 1 piece of bacon or bacon rind

plus:
 2 pt of good quality meat broth
a bunch of chives

Mix flour, milk, eggs and salt to form a smooth batter (not too thick). Heat a heavy frying pan until it is very hot, and grease using the piece of bacon. Pour in some of the batter and spread it over the base of the pan to get a thin pancake – *Flädle*. Repeat until you have used up all the batter. Allow the pancakes to cool, cut in half and then again into thin strips. Add some of the strips to a bowl of very hot meat broth and serve immediately with a sprinkling of chopped chives.

Flädle are one of the ingredients found in traditional "Swabian Wedding Soup". Depending on the region, a long list of additional garnishes are added to the soup e. g. semolina dumplings, beef marrow dumplings, meat balls or liver dumplings, little stuffed noodles, pea shaped baked dumplings, little bits of cooked egg or liver *Spätzle*.
In the past, provincial regulations controlled what could be served at christenings or weddings, limiting them to a one course meal. As a result, the individual courses were especially generous – an interpretation of the law which benefitted the diners!

Saure Kutteln · Sour tripe

Saure Kutteln

1,25 kg vorgekochte Kutteln
400 g Zwiebeln
80–100 g Schweine- oder Butterschmalz
$^3/_4$ l Rotwein (Trollinger oder Lemberger)
1 Schuss Rotweinessig
1 mit 2 Nelken gespickte Zwiebel
2 Lorbeerblätter, 4–5 Wacholderbeeren
einige Pfefferkörner
Salz und frisch gemahlener Pfeffer
Mehlschwitze aus 20 g Butter, 40 g Mehl
4 EL Sauerrahm

Beilage:
Röstkartoffeln (Bratkartoffeln)

Die vorgekochten Kutteln in feine Streifen schneiden, sofern Ihr Metzger das noch nicht getan hat. Die Zwiebeln klein würfeln, im heißen Fett anbraten, dann die Kuttelstreifen zugeben, kurz mitbraten, Wein und Essig zugießen und die Gewürze zugeben. Die Kutteln ca. 30–60 Minuten sanft kochen (je nachdem, wie lange sie vorgekocht waren – am besten einfach probieren). Die Spickzwiebel und die Lorbeerblätter aus der Soße nehmen, mit Salz und Pfeffer abschmecken. Vor dem Anrichten die Mehlschwitze mit dem Sauerrahm und etwas Soße verquirlen und unter die Kutteln rühren. Röstkartoffeln zu den Kutteln servieren.
Kutteln, die man beim Metzger kaufen kann, stammen aus den vier Teilen der Rindermägen. Jeder Teil sieht etwas anders aus – am bekanntesten sind Pansen und Labmagen.
Nicht vorgekochte Kutteln werden mit Wasser, dem ein gehackter Kalbsfuß und ein Teelöffel Natron beigegeben sind, aufgesetzt. Das Natron bewirkt, dass die Kutteln schön hell bleiben. Nach dem ersten Aufkochen wird das Wasser abgegossen und durch neues ersetzt. Nach etwa 4–5 Stunden sind die Kutteln dann soweit, dass sie wie oben beschrieben weiterverarbeitet werden können.

Ochsenmaulsalat

1 Ochsenmaul oder fertig gekochtes
Ochsenmaulfleisch, ausgelöst ca. 600 g

zum Kochen:
Wasser, 1 TL Salz, 1 halbierte Zwiebel

1 milde Gemüsezwiebel

zur Soße:
2–3 EL Weinessig oder
2 EL Weinessig und 1 TL Senf
Salz und weißer Pfeffer, frisch gemahlen
60 ml Ochsenmaul- oder Fleischbrühe
1–2 EL Sonnenblumenöl

Das mehrmals unter lauwarmem Wasser abgewaschene Ochsenmaul mit Salz und der halbierten Zwiebel in ca. 2$^1/_3$ –3 Stunden weich kochen. Noch warm ausbeinen (Knochen auslösen). Bis zum Erkalten zwischen zwei Brettchen leicht pressen.
Gekochtes Ochsenmaul in sehr feine Scheiben schneiden. Die Gemüsezwiebel entweder in halben Scheiben oder fein gehackt zugeben. Die Soße anrühren, pikant abschmecken, mit dem Ochsenmaul vermischen und zum Durchziehen 1 Stunde kühl stellen.
Zum Ochsenmaulsalat schmecken Bratkartoffeln oder Bauernbrot.

Tipps: Beim Metzger gibt es fertig gegartes Ochsenmaulfleisch auf Vorbestellung.
Der fertige Salat kann in einem Steintopf im Keller, gut zugedeckt, etwa 1 Woche aufbewahrt werden. Dann das Öl erst unmittelbar vor dem Anrichten zufügen.

Sour tripe

$2^3/_4$ lb tripe, precooked
14 oz onions
approx 4 oz pork lard or clarified butter
$1^1/_2$ pt red wine (*Trollinger*)
a dash of red wine vinegar
1 onion larded with 1–2 cloves
2 bay leaves
4–5 juniper berries
a few peppercorns
salt and freshly milled pepper

A roux sauce made of:
$^3/_4$ oz butter
$1^1/_2$ oz flour
4 tbsp sour cream

serve with:
fried potatoes

If your butcher has not already done it, cut the
pre-cooked tripe into strips.
Fry the onions in hot fat, then add the tripe.
Fry for a short while, then add the wine, vinegar
and spices. Cook gently for 30–60 minutes,
depending on how long they were pre-cooked
(the best thing is to try them). Remove the larded
onion and the bay leaves from the sauce, and
season with salt and pepper. Before serving, whisk
the sour cream and the roux sauce together with
a little of the sauce and stir into the tripe.
Serve with fried potatoes.
Tripe that can be bought at the butchers comes
from four different parts of the cow's stomach.
Each part looks a little different from the other –
the best known parts are paunch and maw.
If you can only get tripe which has not been pre-
cooked, place it in a pan of water with a chopped
calf's knuckle and a teaspoon of baking soda. The
baking soda prevents the tripe from turning dark
in colour. After the pan has boiled, pour off the
liquid and replace with it with fresh water. After
4–5 hours, the tripe is ready to be used for the
recipe above.

Ox-cheek salad

1 fresh ox cheek or approx $1^1/_4$ lp pre-c
cooked ox-cheek (from your local butcher).

To cook:
water, 1 tsp salt
1 onion, cut in half

1 large mild onion

For the sauce:
2–3 tbsp wine vinegar or
2 tbsp wine vinegar and
1 tbsp mustard, mixed
salt and white pepper, freshly milled
2 fluid oz from cooking the meat, or meat
stock
1–2 tbsp sunflower oil

Wash the ox-cheek under warm running water
several times. Boil for about 2½–3 hours together
with the salt and the onion halves. Debone while
still warm. Place the ox cheek between two
chopping boards with a weight on top and leave
to cool.
Slice the ox-cheek into very fine slices. Add the
mild onion (either finely sliced or diced). Mix
the sauce and season so that it is spicy. Stir into
meat and leave to marinate for an hour in a cool
place.
This tastes good served with fried potatoes
or farmers' bread.

Tips: You can order pre-cooked ox-cheek at your
local butcher.
The prepared salad can be stored in an earthen-
ware pot in a cool place for up to one week. If
you wish to do this, do not add the oil until just
before serving.

Fleischküchle
Meatballs

Fleischküchle

Kartoffelsalat

400 g gemischtes Hackfleisch:
    Rind und Schwein oder nur Rinder-
    hackfleisch
  1 Brötchen vom Vortag, eingeweicht in lau-
    warmes Wasser und dann gut ausgedrückt
  1 Ei, 1 mittelgroße Zwiebel, fein gehackt
1–2 EL Petersilie, fein gehackt
Salz und Pfeffer, frisch gemahlen

nach Belieben:
1–2 Sardellenfilets, fein gewiegt

zum Braten:
  3 EL Sonnenblumenöl, 1 EL Butter

Das Hackfleisch mit dem ausgedrückten klein
gezupften Brötchen, dem Ei, gehacker Zwiebel
und Petersilie vermischen. Nach Belieben würzen
und fein gewiegte Sardellenfilets zugeben. Kleine
runde Fleischküchlein formen, auf der Oberfläche
leicht einkerben. Öl in einer großen Bratpfanne
erhitzen, die Fleischküchle einlegen und von
jeder Seite 5–6 Minuten braten. Zuletzt die Butter
zugeben. Wird Sauce gewünscht, die Fleischküchlein aus der Pfanne nehmen und warm halten.
Den Bratensatz mit ca. $1/8$ Liter Wasser loskochen
und die Soße mit 1 Teelöffel Speisestärke binden.
Dazu gibt es schwäbischen Kartoffelsalat, der
„schlonzig" sein muss.

Anstatt Petersilie kann der Fleischteig auch mit
gezupften Majoranblättchen gewürzt werden.
Dann die Sardellenfilets weglassen. Sollte die
Fleischmasse zu weich sein, kann mit wenig Semmelbröseln und Haferflocken zusätzlich gebunden
werden. Die Fleischküchle konnen auch vor dem
Braten leicht durch Mehl oder Semmelbrösel ge-
zogen werden, dann wird die Kruste knuspriger.

1 kg schmale festkochende Kartoffeln,
    keine mehligen Kartoffeln!
ca. $1/4$ l gut abgeschmeckte Fleischbrühe –
    oder etwas mehr oder heißes
    Wasser, gewürzt mit gekörnter
    Brühe
  1 mittelgroße Zwiebel, fein gehackt
  1 Prise Pfeffer, frisch gemahlen

nach Geschmack:
  $1/2$ TL Salz
4–5 EL Weißweinessig
4–6 EL Sonnenblumenöl

Die Kartoffeln in der Schale kochen. Noch heiß
schälen und dann abkühlen lassen. In feine Scheiben schneiden und in eine Schüssel füllen. Die
Fleischbrühe entfetten, erhitzen und über die
Kartoffelscheiben gießen. Die Menge richtet sich
nach den Kartoffeln, sie sollten „nass" sein. Zwiebelwürfel und Pfeffer zugeben. Mit Salz etwas
vorsichtig sein, da die Fleischbrühe bereits Salz
enthält. Essig untermischen und den Salat für ca.
30 Minuten ruhen lassen. Abschmecken, dann mit
dem Öl mit Hilfe von zwei Gabeln vermischen.

Oder unter den fertigen Kartoffelsalat nur 1 Esslöffel Öl mischen. Ruhen lassen und vor dem Servieren 2–3 Esslöffel zerlassene (nicht braune) Butter darüber träufeln und den Salat mit zwei
Gabeln auflockern.
Schwäbischer Kartoffelsalat wird zimmerwarm
serviert – aus dem Kühlschrank schmeckt er nicht.

Tipp: Bleibt Kartoffelsalat übrig, so kann man ihn
kühl stellen und am nächsten Tag eine Einbrenne
aus Butter und Mehl herstellen. Mit Fleischbrühe
ablöschen, mit 1 Lorbeerblatt und 2 ganzen Nelken
würzen und den Kartoffelsalat darin einmal aufkochen lassen. Dazu schmecken Saiten (Frankfurter-
oder Wiener Würstchen) oder heiße Fleischwurst.

Meatballs

14 oz minced meat (beef and pork mixed or
    else beef only)
1 bread roll from the previous day, soaked
    in lukewarm water and squeezed dry
1 egg, 1 medium onion, finely diced
1–2 tbsp parsley, finely diced
salt and pepper, freshly milled

If you like:
1–2 anchovy fillets, finely chopped

To fry:
3 tbsp sunflower oil
1 tbsp butter

Tear the pre-soaked bread roll into small pieces
and mix with the minced meat, egg, chopped
onions, and parsley. Season to taste and if you
are using them, add the sardine fillets. Shape
to form meat balls. Using a knife, lightly press
the edge into the top of the meat ball. Heat the
oil in a frying pan, add the meatballs and fry for
5–6 minutes. At the end of the frying time, add
the butter. If you want a sauce, remove the
meatballs from the pan and keep them warm.
Deglaze the pan with about ¼ pint of water and
bind with a teaspoon of cornstarch.
Serve with Swabian potato salad which should be
"schlonzig" (sloppy).

Instead of parsley, you can season the meatballs
with marjoram leaves - but then leave out the
sardines. If the meat mixture is too loose, add
a few porridge oats or bread crumbs. If you roll
the meatballs in flour or breadcrumbs before
you fry them, they will be crunchier.

Potato salad

approx 2 lb small hard boiling potatoes –
    don't use the floury type
approx ½ pt well seasoned meat stock
    (depending on the kind of potatoes
    you use)
1 medium sized onion, finely chopped
1 pinch of freshly milled pepper

according to taste:
½ tsp   salt
4–5 tbsp white wine vinegar
4–6 tbsp sunflower oil

Cook the potatoes in their skins. Peel them while
still hot and leave to cool. Cut into fine slices and
place in a bowl. Remove any fat from the meat
stock, heat and pour over the potatoes. How
much you will need, depends on the potatoes –
they should be "wet". Add the diced onions and
the pepper. Be careful when adding the salt, since
the meat stock already contains some. Stir in the
vinegar and leave to marinate for about 30 minutes.
Season and mix in the oil using a fork.

Alternatively, add only 1 tablespoon of oil to the
potato salad. Leave to marinate. Just before serving
pour 2–3 tablespoons of melted butter (not
browned) over the salad and mix using 2 forks.
Swabian potato salad is served at room temperature
– it doesn't taste good fresh from the fridge!

Tip: If you have any leftover potato salad, store it
in a cool place. The next day, make a roux sauce
from butter, flour and meat stock. Add 1 bay leaf
and 2 cloves and bring the potato salad to the
boil in it.
This tastes good served with Frankfurter or
Wiener sausages, or hot meat sausage.

Gaisburger Marsch
oder „Schnitz und Spatzen"
Gaisburg march soup

HÄDECKE

Bücher für
Genießer!

Illustration: Jiří Slíva

H HÄDECKE

Hädecke Verlag GmbH + Co. KG

Tel: +49 (0)70 33 – 1 38 08-0
Fax: +49 (0)70 33 – 1 38 08-13
info@haedecke-verlag.de
www.haedecke-verlag.de

☐ Bitte nehmen Sie mich in Ihren Newsletter-
Verteiler auf! (Versand per E-Mail)

☐ Bitte informieren Sie mich über folgende
Verlagsthemen:

☐ Essen & Trinken   ☐ Gesundheit

Name

Straße

PLZ, Ort

E-Mail (für Newsletter)

Diese Karte entnahm ich dem Buch

Antwort

An den
Hädecke Verlag
Postfach 1203
71256 Weil der Stadt
Deutschland

Bitte
freimachen

Gaisburger Marsch oder „Schnitz und Spatzen"

Zur Brühe:
2 krause Knochen, 1 Markknochen
600 g Rind- oder Ochsenfleisch
(z. B. hohe Rippe, Ochsenbrust, Brustkern,
Bugblatt oder Wade)
1¹/₂–2 l Wasser
1 Gelbe Rübe, ¹/₄ Sellerieknolle
1 Petersilienwurzel 1 kleine Zwiebel
¹/₄ Stange Lauch, 1 EL Salz
einige Pfefferkörner
2 Lorbeerblätter
Spätzle nach dem Rezept Seite 20,
halbe Menge
750 g Kartoffeln

zum Überschmälzen:
geröstete Zwiebelringe
4 EL fein gehackte Petersilie

Die Knochen zerkleinern, mit kaltem Wasser aufsetzen, rasch zum Kochen bringen und dann erst
das Fleisch einlegen. Abschäumen und nach dem
ersten Aufkochen die Hitzezufuhr reduzieren. Die
Brühe sollte nur sanft kochen. Nun das grob zer-
kleinerte Gemüse und die Gewürze zugeben und
die Brühe ca. 1¹/₂–2 Stunden kochen.
In der Zwischenzeit die Spätzle zubereiten und
warm stellen. Die Kartoffeln schälen und in grö-
ßere „Schnitz" schneiden. Die Brühe durch ein
Sieb gießen und die Kartoffelstücke darin
ca. 10–15 Minuten kochen. Das Fleisch solange
warm halten.
Zum Anrichten das Fleisch in kleine Würfel schneiden und abwechselnd mit den Spätzen und den
Kartoffelschnitz in eine vorgewärmte Suppenterri-
ne geben, die heiße Brühe darübergießen. Den
Gaisburger Marsch mit goldgelb gerösteten Zwiebelringen und mit gehackter Petersilie servieren.
Anmerkung: Die Kartoffelschnitz können auch
separat wie Salzkartoffeln gekocht werden – das
spart etwas Zeit. Allerdings dürfen die Stücke
nicht zu gar sein!

In seinem Buch „Preisend
mit viel schönen Reden" schrieb Thaddäus
Troll über den Gaisburger Marsch:
„Eine Leibspeise der Schwaben ist der Gais-
burger Marsch, ein Eintopf aus kleingeschnit-
tenem Ochsenfleisch in einer kräftigen Brühe
mit Kartoffelschnitzen und Spätzle. Vor dem
Ersten Weltkrieg hatten die Einjährigen, die
mindestens sechs Klassen einer höheren Schu-
le besucht haben muss ten, damit automatisch
Offiziersanwärter waren und statt zwei nur ein
Jahr zu dienen hatten, in den Kasernen gewis-
se Vorrechte. So brauchten sie nicht in der
Kantine zu essen, sondern durften in eine
Wirtschaft gehen. Die Einjährigen in der
Stuttgarter Bergkaserne bevorzugten die Küche der Bäckaschmiede in Gaisburg, deren
Spezialität dieser Eintopf war. Vor dem Essen
formierten sie sich zum Gaisburger Marsch,
eine Bezeichnung, die später auf ihr Lieblings-
gericht übertragen worden ist."
Eine der Grundsubstanzen dieses National-
gerichts ist die Kartoffel, die wir den Franzo-
sen zu verdanken haben.
Zehnjährige Steuerfreiheit nebst Grund und
Boden wurde den aus Savoyen wegen ihres
protestantischen Glaubens vertriebenen Wal-
densern in Württemberg zugestanden. Sie
brachten zu Beginn des 18. Jahrhunderts die
Kartoffel und den Maulbeerbaum ins Ländle.
Die 1200 Maulbeerbäume gediehen nicht,
aber die 200 zuerst in Schönenberg bei Maulbronn gepflanzten Kartoffeln eroberten bald
ganz Deutschland.
Sie heißen im Schwäbischen Erdbirnen,
Grundbirnen oder Erdäpfel: Äbira, Grombira,
Ärdäpfl.

Gaisburg march soup

For the soup:

    2 soup bones, 1 marrow bone
    1 lb 6 oz beef or ox meat
$3^{1}/_{2}$–4 pt water
    1 carrot, $^{1}/_{4}$ celleriac bulb
    1 parsley root, 1 small onion
$^{1}/_{4}$ leek stalk
    1 tbsp salt
a few peppercorns
    2 bay leaves
Spätzle (see recipe on page 21)
    – half quantity
$1^{1}/_{2}$ lb potatoes

To garnish:

fried onion rings
    4 tbsp finely chopped parsley

Chop the bones and put them in a pan with some cold water. Quickly bring them to the boil and then add the meat. Ladle off any froth and once the pan comes to the boil again, reduce the heat. The stock should simmer gently. Add the roughly chopped vegetables and the spices, and leave to cook for about $1^{1}/_{2}$ –2 hours.

In the meantime, prepare the *Spätzle* and keep it warm. Peel the potatoes and cut them into large "wedges" (so called „Schnitz"). Pour the meat stock through a sieve and cook the potato wedges in it for about 10–15 minutes. Keep the meat warm. To serve, cut it into small cubes and place a spoon each of *Spätzle*, potatoes and meat cubes in a pre-warmed soup terrine until all of the ingredients are in the terrine. Pour in the meat stock. Serve with golden brown onion rings and chopped parsley.

Comment: To save time, you can cook the potato wedges separately just as you would for boiled salted potatoes, but take care not to overcook them!

In his book „Praise with many fine speeches", Thaddäus Troll (one of the most famous Swabian dialect poets) wrote of Gaisburg march soup, "One of the favourite Swabian meals is the *Gaisburger Marsch*, a soup made of bits of ox-meat in a strong meat broth, with potato wedges and *Spätzle*. Before the First World War, soldiers who had to have attended at least six years of secondary school served in the army for only one year, and were automatically potential officers. They enjoyed special rights in the barracks, one of which was that they did not have to eat in the mess, but were permitted to go to the local inn. The "One Year" soldiers at the Bergkaserne in Stuttgart preferred the food at the "Bäckerschmiede", in Gaisburg, whose speciality was this particular soup. Before going to the inn, the company fell in for the so-called "*Gaisburger Marsch*", or the "march to Gaisburg", a term which latter lent its name to the soup.

One of the main ingredients of this national dish is the potato, something we owe to the French.

At the end of the 17th century, the Protestants, who had been driven out of "Savoyen" for their religious beliefs, settled in Waldenser in Württemberg. There they were granted land, along with ten years exemption from paying taxes, and at the beginning of the 18th century they introduced the potato and the mulberry tree to the region. The 1200 mulberry trees did not flourish, but the more than 200 hundred potato plants that were first planted in Schönenberg, near Maulbronn (famous monatstery, 12th century, near Pforzheim) soon spread throughout most of Germany.

In Swabian, they are known as "earth pears, ground pears or earth apples": *Äbira, Grombira, Ärdäpfl.*

Zwiebelkuchen · Onion cake

Zwiebelkuchen

Hefeteig:
- 10 g frische Hefe
- ca. 1/8 l lauwarme Milch
- 250 g Weizenmehl
- 60 g Schweineschmalz oder Butterschmalz
- 1 Prise Salz,
- 1 Ei

Belag:
- 1 kg Zwiebeln
- 80 g Räucherspeckwürfel oder Grieben
- 30 g Butterschmalz
- 60 g Weizenmehl
- 1/4 l saurer Rahm
- 3–4 Eier, getrennt
- etwas Salz
- 1 EL Kümmel
- Butterflöckchen

Die Hefe zerbröckeln, mit etwas Milch und 2 Esslöffeln Mehl verrühren. Das restliche Mehl in eine Schüssel oder auf ein Backbrett sieben, in die Mitte eine Vertiefung drücken, den Vorteig hineinfüllen und mit etwas Mehl bestäuben. Den Teig an einem warmen, zugfreien Ort so lange gehen lassen, bis die Mehldecke aufreißt. Nun alle übrigen Zutaten mit dem Vorteig gut verarbeiten und den Teig so lange kneten, bis er sich von der Schüssel oder der Hand löst. Den Teig abdecken und so lange gehen lassen, bis er sein Volumen etwa verdoppelt hat. Der Hefeteig kann auch mit Trockenhefe (Anleitung beachten) und mit Hilfe der Küchenmaschine zubereitet werden.
Während der Teig geht, den Belag zubereiten: Die geschälten Zwiebeln klein würfeln, mit den Speckwürfeln oder Grieben im zerlassenen Fett glasig werden lassen. Das Mehl mit dem Rahm glatt rühren, Eigelb, Salz, Kümmel und die abgekühlten Zwiebeln untermischen und zuletzt das steif geschlagene Eiweiß unterziehen. Von der Sahne-Ei-Mischung eine Tasse zurückbehalten. Eine Springform gut fetten, den Hefeteig auswellen, in die Form legen und die Ränder etwas hochziehen. Den Belag gleichmäßig auf dem Teig verteilen, die restliche Sahne-Ei-Mischung darübergeben, Butterflöckchen aufsetzen und den Zwiebelkuchen im vorgeheizten Backofen bei 200–225 °C (Gasherd Stufe 3–4) ca. 35–40 Minuten backen. Zwiebelkuchen schmeckt nur warm! Gut zu Federweißem (neuem Wein) oder Moscht! Zwiebelkuchen kann auch mit Mürbeteig bereitet werden.

Onion cake

Yeast dough:
$1/_2$ oz fresh yeast
approx $1/_4$ pt lukewarm milk
$81/_2$ oz flour
2 oz pork lard or clarified butter
a pinch of salt, 1 egg

Topping:
approx 2 lb onions
$21/_2$ oz diced smoked bacon or graeves
1 oz clarified butter
approx 2 oz flour
$1/_2$ pt sour cream
3–4 eggs, separated
a little salt
1 tbsp caraway
flakes of butter

Crumble the fresh yeast with a little milk and 2 tablespoons of flour. Sieve the rest of the flour into a bowl or a wooden board, make a well in the middle and pour in the yeast mixture, then sprinkle with a little more flour. Stand in a warm, draught free place and leave to rise until the surface of the yeast mixture tears open. Mix all the other ingredients together with the yeast and knead well until the dough comes away from the bowl and your hand easily. Cover the dough and leave to rise until it has doubled in volume. You can also use dried yeast (follow the instructions on the packet). A kitchen machine can be used to make the job easier!

While the dough is rising, prepare the topping. Dice the peeled onions and fry them in the melted fat together with the bacon or graeves until translucent. Mix the flour and the sour cream until smooth, add the egg yolks, salt, caraway and the cooled onions. Finally, fold in the stiffly beaten egg whites. Keep one cup of the topping mix for later.

Grease a loose based cake tin well. Roll out the dough so that it is a little larger than the tin. Line the base, so that the edges of the dough form a ridge around the side. Spread the topping evenly over the dough then cover with the last cup of egg and cream mixture. Dot the surface with the flakes of butter. Bake the onion cake in a preheated oven at 390–435 °F for about 35–40 minutes.

Tips: Onion cake only tastes good served warm! Great with *Federweißer* (new fermenting wine) or *Moscht*!
Onion cake can also be made with shortcrust pastry.

Hefezopf · Plaited yeast bun

Hefezopf

Hefestück:

25 g Frischhefe oder
1 Päckchen Trockenhefe
$^1/_8$–$^1/_4$ l lauwarme Milch
500 g Weizenmehl

weitere Zutaten:

120 g Butter 1 Ei und 2 Eigelb
80 g Zucker
$^1/_2$ TL Salz
abgeriebene Schale von 1 kleinen
unbehandelten Zitrone

nach Belieben:

1 EL Anissamen

zum Bestreichen:

1 Eigelb

zum Bestreuen:

Hagelzucker und Mandelstifte

Die Hefe mit wenig lauwarmer Milch und etwas Mehl zu einem Vorteig anrühren, bedecken und zugfrei warm stellen, damit das Hefestück aufgehen kann. In einer Rührschüssel die Butter schaumig rühren, Ei, Eigelb, Zucker und Salz sowie Zitronenschale und das Hefestück zugeben. Das Mehl in Portionen unterkneten. Soviel Milch zufügen, wie nötig ist, damit ein geschmeidiger Teig entsteht. Den Teig einige Male auf eine Arbeitsfläche schlagen. Dann an der Wärme gehen lassen, bis er das doppelte Volumen erreicht hat. Den Teig in drei Portionen teilen, einzeln auf einem leicht mit Mehl bestäubten Backbrett zu gleich langen Rollen formen. Die Rollen nebeneinander legen und einen Zopf flechten. In der Mitte beginnen und jeweils zu den Enden hin flechten. Die Enden etwas spitz zulaufen lassen und nach unten einschlagen. Den Hefezopf auf ein gefettetes Backblech legen und und nochmals gehen lassen. Mit Eigelb bestreichen und mit Hagelzucker und Mandelstiften bestreuen.
Im vorgeheizten Backofen bei 180°C (Gasherd Stufe 2–3) etwa 30 bis 40 Minuten backen. Die Garprobe mit einem Hölzchen machen!

Tipp: Frischer Hefezopf schmeckt hervorragend, wenn er mit Butter bestrichen und mit einer guten selbst gemachten Konfitüre gekrönt wird. Im Schwabenland heißt Konfitüre „Gsälz". Am liebsten wird Johannisbeer- oder Kirschkonfitüre dazu gegessen.

Plaited yeast bun

For the yeast dough:
   1 oz fresh yeast or 1 packet of dried yeast
$1/4$–$1/2$ pt lukewarm milk
   1 lb flour

Further ingredients:
   4 oz butter
   1 egg and 2 egg yolks
   3 oz sugar
   $1/2$ tsp salt
grated rind of 1 small unwaxed lemon

If required:
   1 tsp anis seeds

For the glaze:
   1 egg yolk

To decorate:
white sugar crystals and almond flakes
or splinters

Mix the yeast with the lukewarm milk and some flour. Cover, and leave to stand in a draught free place so that it can rise. In a mixing bowl, beat the butter until foamy. Add the egg, egg-yolk, sugar, salt, lemon rind and the yeast. Knead in the remaining flour bit by bit. Add enough milk so that you are left with a smooth dough. Beat the dough on the work surface a few times, then leave to rise in a warm place until the dough has doubled in size.

Divide the dough into three pieces. One at a time, form them into long rolls on a floured board. Place the rolls in a row and plait them together (begin in the middle and work outwards toward the ends). Bring the ends together to form a narrow point, and fold them under.

Place the plaited bun on a greased baking tray and leave to rise again. Glaze with egg yolk and sprinkle with the sugar crystals and the almonds. Bake in a pre-heated oven at 355°F for about 30 to 40 minutes. Use a wooden skewer to test it is baked through!

Tip: Freshly baked yeast bun tastes wonderful spread with fresh butter and crowned with some good home made jam. In Swabia, jam is called "Gsälz". Blackcurrant or cherry are the local favourites for this bun.

Dampfnudeln · Steamed yeast dumplings

Ofenschlupfer

3–4 mürbe Äpfel, 40 g Zucker
1–2 EL Arrak oder Rum
6 altbackene Brötchen oder 300 g alt-
backenes Weißbrot
$1/_4$ l Milch, 50 g Butter
5–6 Eier, getrennt
20–30 g Zucker
1 Prise Zimt
abgeriebene Schale von $1/_2$ Zitrone
30–40 g geriebene Mandeln
50 g gewaschene Sultaninen
Butter und Semmelbrösel für die Form
Butterflöckchen zum Aufsetzen
oder 2 Eiweiß(-klar) und 60 g Zucker

Die Äpfel schälen, in feine Blättchen schneiden
und diese mit Zucker und Arrak oder Rum durchziehen lassen.
Die abgeriebenen Brötchen in feine Scheiben
schneiden und mit der Milch anfeuchten. Die Butter schaumig rühren, Eigelb, Zucker, Zimt und Zitronenschale sowie die geriebenen Mandeln dar-
unter rühren. Die Eiklar gesondert zu steifem
Schnee schlagen.
Die Apfelscheiben, die getrockneten Sultaninen
und den Eischnee locker unter die Butter-Eigelb-
Masse heben.
Eine feuerfeste Form ausbuttern, mit Semmelbröseln ausstreuen. Da hinein die Brötchenscheiben
lagenweise mit der Apfelmasse einfüllen, obenauf
reichlich Butterflöckchen setzen. Den Ofenschlupfer in ca. 30–40 Minuten bei 180–200 °C (Gasherd Stufe 2–3) backen – die Oberfläche sollte eine schöne Farbe haben.
Statt Butterflöckchen kann auch Eischnee nach ca.
20 Minuten Backzeit über den Ofenschlupfer ge-
strichen werden. Dazu 2–3 Eiklar mit etwa 60 g
feinem Zucker zu steifem Schnee schlagen. Dann
die Zuckermenge bei den Äpfeln etwas vermin-
dern.

Dampfnudeln

Hefeteig:
500 g Weizenmehl
$1/_2$ Würfel (ca. 20 g frische Hefe)
1 Prise Zucker
$1/_8$–$1/_4$ l lauwarme Milch
2 Eier, 80 g Butter, 60 g Zucker
Schalenabrieb von 1/2 Zitrone
1 Prise Salz

zum Aufziehen (Backen):
40 g Butter, 1 Prise Salz 2 EL Zucker
gut $1/_4$ l Wasser oder halb Milch, halb Wasser

Das Mehl in eine Schüssel oder auf ein Backbrett
schütten und in die Mitte eine Vertiefung drücken.
Die zerbröckelte Hefe, Zucker und etwas Milch
verrühren und in die Vertiefung gießen. Den Vorteig gehen lassen, dann mit allen anderen Zutaten
zu einem geschmeidigen Teig verarbeiten. Den
Teig gehen lassen, dann entweder fingerdick auswellen und mit einem Glas Küchle ausstechen
oder mit einem Löffel kleine Portionen abstechen
(ca. 20 Küchle), nochmals gehen lassen.
In einer Kasserolle die Butter zerlassen, Salz und
Zucker zugeben und die gewünschte Flüssigkeit
(die Flüssigkeit sollte 2 cm hoch in der Kasserolle
stehen). Die Flüssigkeit aufkochen lassen, die
Küchlein hineinsetzen und den Deckel auflegen
(falls der Deckel nicht gut schließt, einen Teigstreifen um den Rand legen). Auf dem Herd bei
mittlerer Hitzezufuhr in ca. 20 Minuten aufziehen.
Wenn die Dampfnudeln aufhören zu zischen,
noch 10 Minuten weiterbacken, damit sich eine
Kruste bildet. Mit einer Backschaufel herausheben
und mit Kompott oder Vanillesoße servieren. Oder
die Dampfnudeln in der offenen Kasserolle im
Backofen bei ca. 180–200 °C in ca. 20–25 Minuten
aufziehen. So bräunen sie ringsum. Evtl. die
Flüssigkeitsmenge erhöhen, damit sie nicht an-
setzen.

Bread and apple pudding (Ofenschlupfer)

3–4 floury apples
1^1/$_2$ oz sugar
1–2 tbsp arrack or rum
   6 old stale bread rolls or 10^1/$_2$ oz stale
     white bread
approx ^{1}/$_2$ pt milk
   2 oz butter
5–6 eggs, separated
2^1/$_2$ tbsp sugar
a pinch of cinnamon
grated rind of ^{1}/$_2$ unwaxed lemon
   2 oz washed raisins
butter and breadcrumbs for the baking dish
1^1/$_2$–2 oz ground almonds
flakes of butter to garnish or 2 egg whites
     and 2½ oz sugar

Peel the apples, and cut them into fine slices.
Leave them to marinate in the sugar and the
arrack or rum.
Grate the crusts off the bread rolls and cut them
into fine slices, then moisten them with milk. Bead
the butter until fluffy, then add the egg yolk, sugar,
cinnamon and lemon rind together with the ground
almonds. Whisk the egg whites separately until stiff.
Fold the apple slices, the dried sultanas and the
egg white into the butter-egg-yolk mixture. Then
grease an oven proof dish with butter, and sprinkle
with bread crumbs. Place the bread slices in layers
with the apple mixture and put plenty of butter
flakes on the top. Bake the apple pudding for
30–40 minutes at 355–390 °F, the surface should
have an attractive golden colour.

Tip: Instead of using flakes of butter, once the
pudding has cooked for about 20 minutes, you
can spread it with stiffly whisked egg whites. Take
2–3 egg whites and whisk them together with
about 2½ oz caster sugar until stiff. Reduce the
amount of sugar you use in the main recipe for
the apples if you want to do this.

Steamed yeast dumplings (Dampfnudeln)

Yeast dough:
   1 lb wheat flour
   ^{1}/$_2$ cube of fresh yeast (approx ^{3}/$_4$ oz)
a pinch of sugar
^{1}/$_2$–^{1}/$_3$ pt lukewarm milk
   2 eggs, 3 oz butter, 2 oz sugar
grated rind of ^{1}/$_2$ unwaxed lemon
a pinch of salt

For baking:
   1^1/$_2$ oz butter
   2 tbsp sugar, a pinch of salt
approx ^{1}/$_2$ pt water, alternatively half
     milk/half water

Place the flour in a bowl or empty it onto on a
wooden board and make a hollow in the middle.
Mix the crumbled yeast with the sugar and some
of the milk and pour the mixture into the hollow.
Leave to rise, then mix together with all the other
ingredients until you have a smooth dough. Leave
the dough to rise, then either roll out to the
thickness of your finger and cut out rounds with
a glass (6–8 cm diameter). Alternatively cut
off portions of the dough with a spoon (approx.
20 dumplings), then leave to rise again.
Melt the butter in a casserole dish, add the salt
and sugar and the required amount of liquid (the
liquid should be about 1 inch deep). Bring to the
boil, put the dumplings into the casserole dish and
seal with a closely fitting lid (if the lid does not
fit tightly, seal the edge of the casserole dish with
a strip of dough). Cook on the stove at medium
heat for about 20 minutes. When the dumplings
stop sizzling, continue to cook them for another
10 minutes so that they form a crust. Remove
them from the pan using a spatula and serve with
compote or vanilla sauce. Alternatively, bake in
the oven without a lid at 355–390 °F for about
20–25 minutes, that way they brown all over.
You may need to use more liquid to prevent them
from sticking.

Ofenschlupfer
Bread and apple pudding

Pfitzauf

5 Eier
250 g Weizenmehl
1 Prise Salz
$^1/_2$ l Milch
125 g Butter
Puderzucker zum Überstäuben

Die Eier mit Mehl, Salz und etwas Milch glattrüh-
ren. Die übrige Milch erhitzen, einen Teil der Butter zum Ausstreichen der Pfitzaufförmchen (Kaf-
feetassen sind auch brauchbar) verwenden, die
restliche Butter in der Milch zerlassen. Die ko-
chend heiße Milch mit der Butter unter den Teig
rühren. Die Förmchen halbvoll mit Teig füllen. Der
Teig geht beim Backen stark auf! Im vorgeheizten
Backofen bei 180 bis 200 °C (Gasherd Stufe 2–3)
etwa 30 bis 40 Minuten backen. Pfitzauf heiß aus
der Form stürzen und zu Kompott, z. B. Apfel-
oder Quittenkompott, oder mit einer Fruchtsoße –
Hägenmarksoße (Hagebuttenmark) passt gut dazu
– servieren.
Werden die Pfitzauf süß serviert, mit etwas Puderzucker überstäuben. Pfitzauf können aber auch als
Beilage zu Gemüse gereicht werden.
Es gibt alte Pfitzaufrezepte, die mehr Mehl (375 g)
und mehr Milch ($^3/_4$ l) sowie 50 g Zucker, dafür
aber weniger Butter vorschreiben. Das rührt unter
anderem daher, dass die früheren Pfitzaufförmchen recht groß waren und dass Pfitzauf als
Hauptgericht gereicht wurde.

Möchte man ein besonders lockeres Ergebnis er-
zielen, so können anstatt 250 g Mehl nur 125 g
Mehl verwendet werden (für 4 kleine Förmchen).
Diese Pfitzauf schmecken köstlich zum Nachtisch
oder zum Nachmittagskaffee.

Holunderküchle

12 gleichgroße schöne Holunderblüten
200 g Mehl
$^1/_4$ l Milch
3 Eier
1 Prise Salz
Butterschmalz zum Ausbacken

Die Holunderblüten waschen und gut ausschüt-
teln. Evtl. auf ein Sieb zum Abtrocknen legen.
Aus Mehl, Milch und Eiern einen Pfannkuchenteig
bereiten, die Holunderblüten am Stiel festhalten,
in den Pfannkuchenteig tauchen und in heißem
Butterschmalz schwimmend goldgelb herausba-
cken. Mit Zimt und Zucker bestreuen und zum
Nachtisch oder Kaffee reichen.
Man kann die Holunderküchle auch ohne Zucker
servieren. Ein Viertele Trollinger passt dann gut
dazu.

Pancake puffs

5 eggs
8½ oz flour
a pinch of salt
1 pt milk
4½ oz butter
icing sugar to decorate

Beat the eggs with the flour, salt and milk until smooth. Heat the rest of the milk, and use some of the butter to grease the baking moulds (you can use oven-proof coffee cups), melt the rest in the warm milk. Once the milk and butter are boiling hot, mix them into the dough. Fill the moulds half full – the dough will rise a lot! Bake in a pre-heated oven at 355–390°F for 30 to 40 minutes.
Tip the puffs out of the moulds while they are still hot and serve them with compote, apricot or quince are good. Alternatively, you can serve them with a fruit sauce such as rosehip.
If you want to serve the pancake puffs as dessert, dust them with icing sugar. They can however be served as a side dish with vegetables.

There are old recipes for pancake puffs that use more flour (13 oz) and more milk (1½ pints) and more sugar (2 oz), but less butter. This is partly because the old pancake puff baking moulds were quite large in the past and the puffs were served as a main course.

If you would like to have particularly light, fluffy results, use 4½ oz of flour instead of 8½ oz (for 4 moulds). These puffs taste delicious as dessert or served with afternoon coffee.

Elder blossom fritters

12 similar sized elder blossoms
7 oz flour
1 pt milk
3 eggs
a pinch of salt
vegetable lard or clarified butter for frying

Wash the blossoms and shake them well till they are dry. Leave them in a colander to drain if necessary.
Make a smooth pancake batter using the flour, eggs and milk. Hold the blossoms by the stalks, dip them one by one in the batter, and fry them in enough hot fat that they float in the pan. Sprinkle with cinnamon and sugar and serve with coffee or as dessert.

You can also serve the elderflower blossoms without sugar, but with a glass of Trollinger (light red wine).

Pfitzauf · Pancake puffs

Gedeckter Apfelkuchen

Für 1 flache Kuchenform Ø ca. 30 cm:
12 Kuchenstücke

Mürbeteig:

280 g Weizenmehl
140 g kalte Butterstückchen
125 g feiner Zucker, 1 Prise Salz
1–2 Eier (je nach Größe)
3–4 EL süße öder saure Sahne

Belag:

1–1,5 kg mürbe nicht zu süße Äpfel
80 g feiner Zucker
Schale und Saft von 1 kleinen Zitrone,
unbehandelt
40 g geschälte, gehackte Mandeln
60 g Sultaninen, mit heißem Wasser
gewaschen und gut abgetropft

zum Bestreichen:

1 Eigelb

Guss:

100 g Butter, 100 g feiner Zucker
1 TL echter Vanillezucker oder
wenig abgeriebene Zitronenschale von
1 unbehandelten Zitrone

Das Mehl auf ein Backbrett häufen, in die Mitte eine Vertiefung drücken. In diese den Zucker, Eier und Sahne geben, die Butterstückchen, Prise Salz auf dem Mehlrand verteilen. Alle Zutaten mit einem großen Messer zuerst vorsichtig, dann energisch zusammenhacken. Rasch zu einem Ball kneten und zugedeckt ca. 30 Minuten kalt stellen. Oder das Mehl in eine Rührschüssel füllen, alle anderen Zutaten darauf geben und mit der Küchenmaschine auf niedriger Schaltstufe verkneten; ebenfalls kalt stellen. Äpfel schälen, zuerst in Achtel, diese in feine Blättchen schneiden. In einer Schüssel mit dem Zucker, Zitronenschale und -saft vermischen und zugedeckt 30 Minuten durchziehen lassen. Aus dem Mürbeteig zwei Böden ausrollen; einer sollte ca. 2 cm größer als die Kuchenform sein. Mit dem größeren Teigboden eine gefettete Form auslegen. Die Apfelblättchen, Mandeln und Sultaninen darauf verteilen, den überstehenden Teigrand zur Mitte hin einschlagen und mit verquirltem Eigelb bestreichen. Den zweiten Teigboden auflegen und ringsum gut andrücken. Für den Guss, die Butter leicht erwärmen, mit Zucker und Vanillezucker oder Zitronenschale vermischen und den Kuchen damit bestreichen. Den Apfelkuchen im vorgeheizten Backofen bei 200 °C (Gasherd Stufe 3) in ca. 35– 45 Minuten hellbraun backen.

Swabian apple pie

Ingredients for 1 cake tin Ø approx 30 cm:
   12 slicese

Shortcrust pastry:
   10 oz flour
   5 oz cold butter pieces
   4 oz caster sugar, a pinch of salt
1–2 eggs (depending on size)
3–4 tbsp sweet or sour cream

Topping:
2–3 lb ripe apples, not too sweet
   3 oz caster sugar
juice and rind of 1 small unwaxed lemon
1$\frac{1}{2}$ oz peeled, chopped almonds
2$\frac{1}{2}$ oz sultanas, washed in hot water and well
   drained

To glaze:
   1 egg yolk

Icing:
approx 4 oz butter, approx 4 oz caster sugar
1 tsp genuine vanilla sugar, or a little lemon
   rind from an unwaxed lemon

Place the flour on a wooden board. Make a small hollow in the middle and pour in the sugar, eggs and cream. Sprinkle the edge of the flour with a pinch of salt and place the pieces of butter around the top of the pile.
Using a large knife, carefully chop the mixture together. Once the dough starts to come together you can work faster. Quickly knead together to form a ball and leave to chill for 30 minutes. Alternatively, place all the other ingredients for the dough in a bowl, and use a electric mixer at slow speed to prepare it.
Chill as before.
Peel the apples and cut them into quarters, then again into eighths. Cut each of these pieces into thin slices and place in a bowl together with the sugar, and the rind and juice of the lemon. Leave to marinate for 30 minutes.
Roll the dough out into two round pieces, one of which should be ¾ inch larger than the cake tin. Use the larger piece to line the greased baking tin. Spread with the apples, chopped almonds and sultanas and then fold over the rim of the dough towards the middle and glaze with beaten egg yolk. Place the second round of pastry on top and press the edges down well to seal the pie.
For the icing, gently heat the butter. Mix with the sugar and the vanilla sugar, or lemon rind, and spread over the pie.
Bake in a pre-heated oven at 390 °F for approx. 35–45 minutes until golden brown.

Weinberg mit Blick auf den Neckar bei Mundelsheim
Vineyard with a view of the river Neckar near Mundelsheim
(Werbegemeinschaft Württembergischer Weingärtnergenossenschaften)

Weinland Württemberg
Wine Country Württemberg

Steillagen, Terrassen- oder Hanglagen sind typisch für den württembergischen „Wengert", den Weingarten, der vom Weingärtner, dem „Wengerter" mit Fachkenntnis und Erfahrung gepflegt wird. Kein Wunder, dass die Schwaben ihren Wein am liebsten „selber schlotzen" und der Württemberger Wein zu den begehrten Raritäten zählt. Dabei sind die Erträge des Landes nicht eben gering: Württemberg ist Deutschlands fünftgrößtes Weinbaugebiet und reicht vom Taubergrund bis zum Albtrauf. Der Weinbau verteilt sich auf die beiden Zentren um Stuttgart und Heilbronn und auf die sonnigen Lagen des Neckartals und der Täler der Nebenflüsse Rems, Murr, Enz, Bottwar, Zaber, Kocher und Jagst. Die landschaftliche Vielfalt spiegelt sich in 16 Großlagen und 203 Einzellagen wider, deren reichhaltiges Rebsortiment einmalig für Deutschland ist.

Das schwäbische Nationalgetränk unter den Weinen ist der *Trollinger* (der Name geht auf Tirol, „Tyrolinger", zurück), eine spätreifende Rotweinsorte, die auf nährstoffreichen Böden und in besten Hanglagen gedeiht. Der herzhaft-kernige Charakter des Weins passt gut zu herzhaft-rustikalen Speisen wie Rostbraten, Linsen, Spätzle und Saiten oder zu Kutteln, wobei die Zugabe von Trollinger zum „Sößle" den Gerichten nicht schadet.

Zu den Roten gehört auch der leuchtend rote, harmonisch-gehaltvolle *Schwarzriesling*, der gut zu Wild und Geflügel passt, und der anspruchsvolle *Spätburgunder*, ein purpurrotes, körperreiches Spitzengewächs (gut zu Wild- und Rindgerichten). Längst kein Geheimtipp mehr ist eine originäre Züchtung aus Württemberg, der *Dornfelder*, ein farbintensiver, kräftiger Rotwein, der sich hervorragend zum Ausbau im Barrique (Eichenholzfass) eignet. Eine selten gepflegte Spielart aus der Burgunderfamilie ist der *Klevner* und seit einiger Zeit macht der *Samtrot* von sich reden, eine Abwandlung des *Schwarzrieslings*, der mit warmem Rotton und samtiger Fülle seinem Namen alle Ehre macht. Zur Elite der Rotweinsorten zählt der *Lemberger*, ein höchst anspruchsvolles Gewächs, was Lage, Klima und Boden angeht. Daher wird es auch nur in begrenztem Umfang angebaut – aber was für ein Getränk! Der krönende Höhepunkt zu Wild- und Pilzgerichten.

Auch mit ihren Weißweinen müssen sich die schwäbischen Wengerter nicht vor der Konkurrenz verstecken. Auf den schweren Keuper- und Muschelkalkböden des Landes wächst ein eleganter *Riesling* mit dezentem Bukett und pikanter Säure, der gut zu Fisch und Meeresfrüchten passt, den man aber unbedingt auch einmal zum Zwiebelkuchen oder Hefezopf probieren sollte. Letzteres gilt auch für den *Gewürztraminer*, der nur in den besten Lagen des Landes angebaut wird. Er ist ein idealer Begleiter zu Desserts und würzigem Käse. Leichter und duftiger ist der *Müller-Thurgau*, der sich gut zu Vorspeisen, Suppen und Desserts eignet. Dazu passt auch der leichte, unaufdringliche *Silvaner*, der in den Tallagen rund um Heilbronn und Weinsberg und auf den Keuperböden des Hohenloher Landes gut gedeiht.

Ein echter Schwabe und originär württembergische Züchtung ist der *Kerner*, der aus der Kreuzung zwischen *Trollinger*- und *Rieslingrebe* entstand. Mit feinrassiger Säure und kraftvollem Körper ist er von unverwechselbarem, eigenwilligen Charakter – wie sein Namenspatron, der Arzt und Dichter Justinus Kerner. Noch ein schwäbischer Dichter ist Namenspatron für eine württembergische Spezialität: Der frische, leichte *Schiller* wird aus gemeinsam gekelterten blauen, roten und weißen Trauben aller in Württemberg angepflanzten Rebsorten gewonnen und verfügt somit über eine Fülle verschiedenster Geschmackskomponenten. Er passt wunderbar zu Fisch, Gemüse und Geflügel. Nicht zu verwechseln ist der Schiller mit dem Weißherbst, dessen Trauben nur von einer Rebsorte stammen dürfen und im Unterschied zum Rotwein sofort nach der Lese gekeltert werden. So entsteht die typische hellrote Farbe.

Der Schwabe liebt sein „Viertele", und das wird als Trollinger, im „Vierteles"glas mit Henkel serviert. Das weiße Viertele kommt dagegen in einer schwäbischen Weinwirtschaft gut gekühlt im „Römer" auf den Tisch. Apropos Weinwirtschaft: Viele werden von den Wengertern selbst geführt, man wird ehrlich, schwäbisch-freundlich-deftig bedient, etwa nach dem Motto: „So, send'r wiader z'faul zom Kocha gwea!" Aber das ist eine andere Geschichte und würde den Rahmen unseres Buches sprengen …

Steep slopes, terraces and hillsides are typical locations for the *Wengert*, (vineyards) of Württemberg. Meticulously cared for by experienced and knowledgeable wine growers, Württenberg wines are a sought after rarity outside the region. Not that they produce small quantities: Württemberg is Germany's fifth largest wine producing region, one that reaches from Taubergrund to the Albtrauf; but the wine is so good, that the Swabians like to keep it for themselves.

Wine production is concentrated in the regions around Stuttgart and Heilbronn, as well as the sunny slopes of the Neckar valley and the valleys of its tributaries; the Rems, Murr, Enz, Bottwar, Zabar, Kocher and Jagst. This geographical diversity is reflected in the 16 regional sites and the 203 individual wine locations, whose wide range of grape varieties is unique in Germany. The Swabian national favourite is *Trollinger*, a late-ripening, red grape which flourishes on rich soils and the best situated slopes, (the name stems from Tirol in Austria, "Tirolinger" and means "from Tirol").

The hearty, full-bodied character of the wine goes well with the down-to-earth, rustic foods of the region, like Swabian pork steaks, lentils, *Spätzle* and sausages, or tripe – where a drop of *Trollinger* in the sour sauce never hurts!

Other reds from the region include *Schwarzriesling*, a rich, harmonious, bright-red coloured wine, ideal served with game and poultry, and *Spätburgunder*, a first-class, full-bodied grape (good with game and beef), with a purplish-red colour.

The native *Dornfelder* variety – no longer an insider tip – is an intense, strong red wine, ideally suited to maturing in barrique oak barrels.

Klevner is a rare burgundy; and the much talked about *Samtrot* (Velvet Red), a variation of the *Schwarzriesling*, which with its warm red tones and velvety body certainly does its name justice, can both be added to the list.

Lemberger counts as one of the regions top wines, a demanding grape that requires a very specific combination of location, climate and soil. As a result, it is only cultivated in a few places: but what a wine! The crowning highlight of any meal when served with game and mushroom dishes.

The region's wine growers have nothing to fear from the competition when it comes to their white wines. The heavy keuper and limestone soils in the region produce an elegant Riesling with a subtle bouquet and zesty acidity that is good with fish and seafood. But has to be tasted at least once with onion cake or plaited yeast bun. The same goes for Gewürztraminer, which is only grown on the best slopes in the state, an ideal accompaniment to dessert and strong cheeses. *Müller-Thurgau* is a lighter and more fragrant wine, well suited to starters, soups and desserts; as is the light and subtle *Silvaner*, which flourishes on the keuper soils in the Hohenlohe area, and in the valleys around Heilbronn and Weinsberg,

A true Swabian and original Wurttemberg grape variety is the *Kerner*, a hybrid of the *Trollinger* and *Riesing* grape varieties.

Its fine acidity plus its strong body have an unmistakeable, individual character – just like its namesake, the doctor and poet Justinus Kerner. There is another Swabian poet who lends his name to a Württemberg speciality: the fresh, light *Schiller* wine is produced from a mix of blue, red and white grapes all grown in the region, pressed together at the same time, resulting in a complex and varied taste. It harmonizes with fish, vegetables and poultry. *Schiller* should not be confused with *Weissherbst*, where only one variety of grape is used, and which unlike red wine is pressed immediately after picking. This is where the wine gets its typical light red colour.

The Swabians love their *Viertele* (¼ litre – ½ pint, measure of wine), and the *Trollinger* is served in a "*Viertele*" glass – a special wine glass with a handle. However, in real Swabian taverns, a white wine "*Viertele*" is served in a so called "*Römer*" (so called "Roman", a traditional wine glass with a coloured glass stem).

Talking of wine taverns: Many of them are run by the wine growers themselves. The service here is straightforward and Swabian: friendly and down to earth, and you can expect comments like: "So, too lazy to cook yourself today, are you?" But that's another story, one that's beyond the scope of this book for now …